GEOGRAPHY IN CLASSICAL ANTIQUITY

GW00676507

What were the limits of knowledge of the physical world in Greek and Roman antiquity? How far did travellers reach and what did they know about far-away regions? How did they describe foreign countries and peoples? How did they measure the earth, and distances and heights upon it? Did they use maps? Ideas about the physical and cultural world are the key to understanding ancient history, but until now there has been no up-to-date introduction to ancient geography. Employing a variety of sources – philosophical and scientific texts, poems and travelogues, papyri and visual evidence – this book explores the origins and development of geographical ideas in classical antiquity and the techniques for describing landscape, topography and ethnography.

DANIELA DUECK is a Senior Lecturer in the Departments of History and Classical Studies at Bar Ilan University. She is the author of *Strabo of Amasia: A Greek Man of Letters in Augustan Rome* (2000) and co-editor (with Hugh Lindsay and Sarah Pothecary) of *Strabo's Cultural Geography: The Making of a* Kolossourgia (2005). She is interested in ancient geography and ethnography and is currently conducting a research project on geographical fragments supported by the Israel Science Foundation.

KAI BRODERSEN is President of the University of Erfurt and holds the Chair of Ancient Culture. He has published extensively on classical inscriptions, oracles and paradoxography and on Greek and Roman historiography, geography and cartography.

KEY THEMES IN ANCIENT HISTORY

EDITORS

P.A. Cartledge
Clare College, Cambridge
P.D.A. Garnsey
Jesus College, Cambridge

Key Themes in Ancient History aims to provide readable, informed and original studies of various basic topics, designed in the first instance for students and teachers of Classics and Ancient History, but also for those engaged in related disciplines. Each volume is devoted to a general theme in Greek, Roman, or where appropriate, Graeco-Roman history, or to some salient aspect or aspects of it. Besides indicating the state of current research in the relevant area, authors seek to show how the theme is significant for our own as well as ancient culture and society. By providing books for courses that are oriented around themes it is hoped to encourage and stimulate promising new developments in teaching and research in Ancient History.

Other books in the series

Death-Ritual and Social Structure in Classical Antiquity, by Ian Morris
978 0 521 37465 0 (hardback), 978 0 521 37611 4 (paperback)

Literacy and Orality in Ancient Greece, by Rosalind Thomas
978 0 521 37346 8 (hardback), 978 0 521 37742 0 (paperback)

Slavery and Society at Rome, by Keith Bradley
978 0 521 37287 9 (hardback), 978 0 521 36887 7 (paperback)

Law, Violence, and Community in Classical Athens, by David Cohen
978 0 521 38167 3 (hardback), 978 0 521 38837 6 (paperback)

Public Order in Ancient Rome, by Wilfried Nippel
978 0 521 38327 7 (hardback), 978 0 521 38749 3 (paperback)

Friendship in the Classical World, by David Konstan
978 0 521 45402 6 (hardback), 978 0 521 45998 2 (paperback)

Sport and Society in Ancient Greece, by Mark Golden
978 0 521 49698 5 (hardback), 978 0 521 49790 6 (paperback)

Food and Society in Classical Antiquity, by Peter Garnsey
978 0 521 64182 9 (hardback), 978 0 521 64588 3 (paperback)

Banking and Business in the Roman World, by Jean Andreau
978 0 521 38031 6 (hardback), 978 0 521 38932 1 (paperback)

Roman Law in Context, by David Johnston
978 0 521 630460 (hardback), 978 0 521 63961 1 (paperback)

Religions of the Ancient Greeks, by Simon Price
978 0 521 38201 7 (hardback), 978 0 521 38867 8 (paperback)

Christianity and Roman Society, by Gillian Clark
978 0 521 63310 9 (hardback), 978 0 521 63386 9 (paperback)

Trade in Classical Antiquity, by Neville Morley
978 0 521 63279 9 (hardback), 978 0 521 63416 8 (paperback)

Technology and Culture in Greek and Roman Antiquity, by Serafina Cuomo
9780 521 81073 9 (hardback), 9780 521 00903 4 (paperback)

Law and Crime in the Roman World, by Jill Harries
9780 521 82820 8 (hardback), 9780 521 53532 8 (paperback)

The Social History of Roman Art, by Peter Stewart
9780 521 81632 8 (hardback), 9780 521 01659 9 (paperback)

Asceticism in the Graeco-Roman World, by Richard Finn
9780 521 86281 3 (hardback), 9780 521 68154 4 (paperback)

Ancient Greek Political Thought in Practice, by Paul Cartledge
9780 521 45455 1 (hardback), 9780 521 45595 4 (paperback)

Money in Classical Antiquity, by Sitta von Reden
9780 521 45337 0 (hardback), 9780 521 45952 5 (paperback)

An Environmental History of Ancient Greece and Rome, by Lukas Thommen
9781 107 00216 6 (hardback), 9780 521 17465 7 (paperback)

Geography in Classical Antiquity, by Daniela Dueck and Kai Brodersen
9780 521 19788 5 (hardback), 9780 521 12025 8 (paperback)

GEOGRAPHY IN CLASSICAL ANTIQUITY

DANIELA DUECK

WITH A CHAPTER BY

KAI BRODERSEN

CAMBRIDGE UNIVERSITY PRESS
Cambridge, New York, Melbourne, Madrid, Cape Town,
Singapore, São Paulo, Delhi, Mexico City

Cambridge University Press
The Edinburgh Building, Cambridge CB2 8RU, UK

Published in the United States of America by Cambridge University Press, New York

www.cambridge.org
Information on this title: www.cambridge.org/9780521120258

© Cambridge University Press 2012

First published 2012

Printed in the United Kingdom at the University Press, Cambridge

A catalogue record for this publication is available from the British Library

ISBN 978-0-521-19788-5 Hardback
ISBN 978-0-521-12025-8 Paperback

Contents

vii

Figures

Acknowledgements

Several people supported and actively helped in producing this book. We owe deep gratitude to Michael Sharp for the first suggestion that we should write it and for his patient guidance throughout all phases of writing and production. Paul Cartledge and Peter Garnsey read the text and meticulously commented on it and groomed it. We benefited enormously from the insightful comments on earlier versions of the manuscript offered by several anonymous readers as well as by Joseph Geiger. We would also like to thank Douglas Olson for his contribution to the refinement of our English. Finally, thanks are due to Tal Relles-Shorer for her technical assistance.

Unless otherwise indicated, translations of literary texts in this book are slightly modified versions of the Loeb Classical Library editions where available.

Chronology

Date	Authors	Texts	Events
BCE			
17th–13th centuries		Linear B ('Pylian geography')	
8th century	[Homer] (*c.* 700)	*Iliad* and *Odyssey*	Beginning of Greek colonization in the Mediterranean and the Black Sea
7th century	Aristeas of Proconnesus (*c.* 675)	*Arimaspea*	Aristeas travels north of the Black Sea; reaches the Sea of Azov
6th century		First *periploi* Massaliote *periplous*	*c.* 600 Necho II of Egypt digs a canal from the Nile to the Arabian Gulf; he sends a Phoenician expedition to circumnavigate Africa
	Scylax of Caryanda (*c.* 515)	*Periplous of places outside the Pillars of Hercales periodos gês*	Euthymenes explores the west coast of Africa
	Hecataeus of Miletus (*c.* 550–490)	*periodos gês* or *periêgêsis*	*c.* 515 Scylax of Caryanda is sent by Darius I to sail down the Indus river and circumnavigate Arabia
			c. 500 Hanno of Carthage sails along the Atlantic coasts of Africa
			c. 500 Himilco of Carthage sails along the Atlantic coasts of Europe
5th century	Herodotus of Halicarnassus (*c.* 484–*c.* 428)	*History*	Xerxes sends Sataspes to circumnavigate Africa Athenian League spreads in the Aegean
	[Hippocrates] (469–399)	*On Airs, Waters, Places*	

x

Date	Authors	Texts	Events
	Ctesias of Cnidus (late 5th century)	*Persika* *Indika* *Periplous*	
4th century	Xenophon (*c.* 428–*c.* 354)	*Anabasis*	*c.* 401 Greek mercenaries' journey from inner Asia to the Greek mainland
	Ephorus of Cyme (*c.* 405–330)	*Histories*	Campaigns of Alexander the Great
	Nearchus of Crete (*c.* 360–295)	Description of India *Periplous* of his voyage	Nearchus of Crete sails from India to the Persian Gulf Pytheas' journey to the North Atlantic
	Onesicritus of Astypalaea (*c.* 360–290)	Description of India	
	Megasthenes (*c.* 350–290)	*Indika*	
	Ophelas of Cyrene (*fl. c.* 320–310)	*Periplous* of the Atlantic coast of Africa	
	Pytheas of Massalia (*fl. c.* 310–306)	*On the Ocean*	
	[Pseudo-Scylax]	*Periplous* of the Mediterranean and the Black Sea	
		Partial Greek translation of Hanno's voyage	
3rd century	Dicaearchus of Messana (340–290)	*periodos gês*	*c.* 284 Patrocles, admiral of Seleucus I, explores the Caspian Sea
	Hecataeus of Abdera (*c.* 323–290)	*Aigyptiaka*	Demodamas, a military commander of Seleucus and Antiochus, crosses the Jaxartes
	Apollonius of Rhodes (*c.* 295–*c.*246)	*Argonautica*	241 End of First Punic War; Rome annexes Sicily
	Eratosthenes of Cyrene (*c.* 276–195)	*Geographika* *On the Measurement of the Earth*	
	Polybius (*c.* 200–118)	*Histories* On living conditions in the equatorial region	

Date	Authors	Texts	Events
2nd century	Agatharchides of Cnidus (*c.* 200–140)	*Periplous* of the Erythraean Sea	*c.* 150 Crates of Mallus displays his globe in Pergamum with four *oikoumenai* on it
	Hipparchus of Nicaea (*c.* 190–126)	*Against the Geography of Eratosthenes*	Ptolemy VIII sends Eudoxus of Cyzicus to explore the route between Egypt and India; he attempts the
	Artemidorus of Ephesus (*c.* 100)	Description of the world	circumnavigation of Africa
1st century		[Anonymous], Geography in iambic trimeters dedicated to Nicomedes of Bithynia ('Pseudo-Scymnus') (*c.* 100)	26–24 Aelius Gallus, the Roman governor of Egypt, explores Arabia and Ethiopia 19 L. Cornelius Balbus, defeats the Saharan tribe of the Garamantes
	Posidonius of Apamea (*c.* 135–*c.* 50)	*On the Ocean*	
	Dionysius son of Calliphon (*c.* 100–87 BCE)	Description of Greece	
	Xenophon of Lampsacus (100–60 BCE)	*Periplous* of the coasts of northern and western Europe	
	Julius Caesar (100–44)	*Gallic War*	
	Varro Atacinus (82–30)	*Argonautica* *Chorographia*	
	Alexander 'Lychnus' of Ephesus (75–45)	Geographical epics	
	M. Vipsanius Agrippa (*c.* 64–12)	Geographical commentary	
	Menippus of Pergamum (*fl. c.* 20)	*Periplous* of the inner sea (Mediterranean)	
	Isidorus of Charax (*c.* 40–1)	*Stathmoi Parthikoi (Parthian Stations)*	

Date	Authors	Texts	Events
CE			
1st century	Strabo of Amasia (64 BCE-23 CE)	*Geography*	Consolidation of the Roman Empire under Augustus
	Iouba II of Mauretania (*c.* 50 BCE–23 CE)	*Libyaka* *Assyriaka* *Arabika* Commentary on Hanno's voyage	43 Claudius' campaign in Britain
	Augustus (63 BCE–14 CE)	*Res Gestae*	
	Pomponius Mela (*fl.* 43/44)	*De chorographia*	
		Stadiasmus Provinciae Lyciae (*c.* 43)	
	Pliny the Elder (*c.* 23–79)	*Natural History*	
	[Anonymous] (mid 1st century)	*Periplus Maris Erythraei*	
	C. Valerius Flaccus (*fl.* 80–92)	*Argonautica*	
	Cornelius Tacitus (*c.* 55–120)	*Agricola* *Germania* *Histories* *Annals*	
2nd century	Claudius Ptolemaeus (*c.* 90–168)	*Almagest* *Geography*	101–106 Trajan's victories over Dacia
	Dionysius of Alexandria (*fl.* 130–138)	Poetic description of the world (hexameters)	
	Arrian (120–170)	*Periplous* of the Black Sea	
	Pausanias of Magnesia (*fl. c.* 150–180)	*Periegesis Hellados (Description of Greece)*	
		Forma Urbis Romae (*c.* 200)	
3rd century	Iunius Solinus (*fl. c.* 300)	*Collectanea Rerum Memorabilium*	
		Tabula Peutingeriana (*c.* 300?)	
		Antonine Itinerary	

Date	Authors	Texts	Events
4th century	Theophanes of Hermopolis (*c.* 320)	*Itinerarium* to and from Antioch	
		[Anonymous], *Itinerarium Burdigalense* or *Itinerarium Hierosolymitanum* (*c.* 333)	
	Postumius Rufius Festus Avienus (340–380)	*Descriptio Orbis Terrae* *Ora Maritima*	
	Marcianus of Heraclea (*c.* 400)	*Periplous* of the Outer Sea	
6th century	Stephanus of Byzantium	*Ethnika*	

Abbreviations

AE	*L'Année Épigraphique*
AHB	*Ancient History Bulletin*
AJA	*American Journal of Archaeology*
AJPh	*American Journal of Philology*
AncSoc	*Ancient Society*
AncW	*The Ancient World*
ANRW	*Aufstieg und Niedergang der römischen Welt*, 1972–
BICS	*Bulletin of the Institute of Classical Studies*
C&M	*Classica et Mediaevalia*
CIL	*Corpus Inscriptionum Latinarum*, 1863–
ClAnt	*Classical Antiquity*
CPh	*Classical Philology*
CQ	*Classical Quarterly*
CRAI	*Comptes rendus de l'Académie des Inscriptions et Belles-Lettres*
DHA	*Dialogues d'histoire ancienne*
FGrHist	F. Jacoby, *Fragmente der griechischen Historiker*, Berlin, 1923–
G&R	*Greece and Rome*
GGM	C. Müller, *Geographi Graeci Minores*, Paris, 1855–1861
GLM	A. Riese, *Geographi Latini Minores,* Heilbronn, 1878
GRBS	*Greek, Roman and Byzantine Studies*
HSPh	*Harvard Studies in Classical Philology*
JAOS	*Journal of the American Oriental Society*
JARCE	*Journal of the American Research Center in Egypt*
JEA	*Journal of Egyptian Archaeology*
JHS	*Journal of Hellenic Studies*
JRA	*Journal of Roman Archaeology*
JRS	*Journal of Roman Studies*
LEC	*Les études classiques*

LSJ	H.G. Liddell, R. Scott and H.S. Jones, *A Greek–English Lexicon*, 9th edn., Oxford, 1996
RE	*Paulys Real-encyclopaedie der Klassischen Altertumswissenschaft*, Stuttgart and Munich, 1894–
REA	*Revue des études anciennes*
REL	*Revue des études latines*
RhM	*Rheinisches Museum für Philologie*
RIB	R.G. Collingwood and R.P. Wright, *The Roman Inscriptions of Britain*, Oxford, 1965–
SCI	*Scripta Classica Israelica*
SEG	*Supplementum Epigraphicum Graecum*, 1923–
SH	*Supplementum Hellenisticum*
TAPhA	*Transactions of the American Philological Association*

CHAPTER I

Introduction

I.I OUTLINE AND GOALS

Today one can remain comfortably at home and, with a single click of the mouse, take a detailed look at a street-corner in a city on the other side of the world, examine a river delta in a remote continent, or learn the dimensions of a mountain hundreds of kilometres away. In antiquity, an age when individuals rarely left their birthplace, horizons were narrow and bounded by unknown and frightening regions, and instruments were simple. How could men discover that the earth was round? How did they estimate its size? How did traders and settlers look for new territory in unknown regions? How did generals set out with armies from Greece to Iran or India? The Greeks and Romans did all that and more, and produced achievements that in many ways still form the basis of our own ideas of geography.

Geography – literally a written or drawn description of the earth (*gê*) – always and everywhere originates in an awareness of one's own surroundings, in encounters with foreign places and peoples and, like any human realm of knowledge, in simple curiosity and the wish to define observed phenomena. These three motives – awareness, encounters and curiosity – must have existed in the early periods of Greek cultural formation, and persisted in various degrees throughout antiquity. Greek studies of landscapes and the environment, along with an interest in remote regions and ideas about the shape of the earth, prevailed long before these issues were recognized as a discipline.

Not only did the ancients lack a clear disciplinary definition of geography,[1] but there were no geographers and geographies in the sense of specialized authors and works with clear, specific characteristics and qualifications. Geographical themes appeared in almost every literary

---

[1] The adjective *geôgraphikos* is first attested in Eratosthenes (third century BCE). See LSJ, s.v.

genre, and works devoted exclusively and consciously to geographical issues might be written in prose or verse, discuss the world as a whole or a region within it, or deal with either concepts or calculations (1.2). No specific skills were required of authors of 'geographies': poets, historians, travellers and philosophers all dealt with geographical matters. Moreover, in the education of the Greek and Roman upper classes, children and adolescents did not study geography for its own sake – geometry and astronomy formed part of a higher stage of education – but only in its Homeric context, as a mixture of fact and fiction, or as the backdrop for historical events, mainly wars.[2]

Despite the absence of an ancient discipline of geography, the words 'geography' and 'geographical' cannot be avoided in modern discussions of classical notions of space, landscape and environment. The use must be refined or modified in contexts where there is a risk of ambiguity, and the reader must be trusted to be able to distinguish between the modern concept and the ancient one.

Like other fields of enquiry in antiquity, geographical writings were both produced and read by a limited social circle. An individual had to be literate to compose reports of travel experiences, and well educated to discuss scientific theories and observations. Advanced mathematical and astronomical skills were needed, particularly in the scientific and carto-graphic branches of geography. Finally, once completed, works had to be accessible both physically (copies) and cognitively (literacy) in order to spread the word or image (if maps were in question). Although it is difficult to assess the situation precisely, the extent of geographical knowledge among illiterate and common people seems to have been limited (5.2). Oral expressions, for example by merchants and soldiers, or public monuments such as inscriptions and sculptures, must have been available to a wide public. But even these probably created only amorphous ideas of remote lands and nations, rather than a coherent concept of the world. For the ordinary person, such ignorance probably did not matter much. Things were different, however, in the case of a military leader or a merchant who had no idea where he was, where he was going, how long his march or voyage was going to be, and what conditions he was likely to have to confront.

Three major historical processes influenced the development of geography in classical antiquity: (1) the Greek 'colonization' of the Archaic

---

[2] Marrou (1965), 265–279; Rawson (1985); Morgan (1998), esp. 33–39. History too was never studied as a discipline. For the geographical knowledge of ordinary people, see 5.2.

period (eighth–sixth centuries BCE); (2) the campaigns of Alexander the Great and the eastward expansion of the Greek world (fourth century BCE); and (3) the consolidation of the Roman Empire, particularly in the time of Augustus (first century CE), but also under the emperors Claudius and Trajan. All three processes significantly promoted territorial expansion, increasing awareness of previously unknown far-away regions of the world, as well as fostering a richer acquaintance with nearer ones. These three waves led to the documentation of new experiences, producing literary genres and enhancing trends within the development of geography. None of this means that geographical interest froze or declined in other periods. As we will see, intellectual processes of this sort were constant throughout antiquity. But the expansion of physical horizons directly and unsurprisingly influenced the extent of knowledge of the world, while creating new intellectual problems and producing novel solutions to old ones.

This book offers a brief introduction to ancient Greek and Roman geography, from its known beginnings in the Archaic era to the late Roman Empire.[3] We survey the surviving literature to present the extent of ancient geographical knowledge as reflected by changing borders and widening horizons, with an eye to the original contexts and formats of geographical records and presentation.

Because of the particular nature of ancient geographical sources, we have rejected chronological order as a primary organizing criterion. Instead, the discussion that follows is divided into three groups of records corresponding to three ancient approaches to the theme: (1) the descriptive, verbal and literary approach; (2) the scientific, mathematical, accurate method; and (3) the (carto)graphic, visual technique. Sections in one chapter occasionally overlap chronologically with those in others, presenting simultaneous transformations and developments. In addition, some texts and authors are relevant to more than one context and are cited in accordance with the needs of the discussion.

Although the verbal, descriptive species of literary geography (chapter 2) was methodologically very different from the mathematical and scientific approach (chapter 3), it was not necessarily fictional. Developing mainly in the form of geographical digressions within historiographical works, it supplied the 'true' picture of venues of attested events, and it is reasonable

---

[3] Earlier surveys of ancient geography, some outdated, others offering only a partial picture, include: Bunbury (1883); Tozer (1897); Warmington (1934); Thomson (1948); Van Paassen (1957); Aujac (1975); Pédech (1976); Dion (1977); Prontera (1983); Jacob (1991); Cordano (1992).

to assume that it was accessible to a wider audience than the more strictly scientific approach. Science began with the naturalistic discussions of the Presocratic philosophers, who offered theories about the structure and essence of the universe and the physical layout of the world, including its shape, size, boundaries and inhabitants. From these roots grew mathematical geography, which attempted to define the earth through precise calculation. The scientific approach produced written records, but also paved the way for initial attempts to represent portions of the world graphically (chapter 4).

Several elements were to make up the backbone of ancient geography. Appreciation of these is sharpened through comparison with parallel experiences and practices of modern geography:[4]

Necessity. Geographical interests emerged in the Greek world from daily needs. Because the Greeks lived around the Mediterranean and Black Sea and relied on maritime transportation for warfare and commerce, they needed information about sea-routes and foreign countries. Similarly, geography supplied the Romans with details necessary for military purposes and administrative functions, while the growing traffic of men and merchandise created a demand for accurate travel information. Unlike the academic and theoretical interest inherent in much modern geography, ancient geography was tied directly to everyday life, and was based not on research by highly qualified 'geographers', but on the experience of ordinary eyewitnesses.

Concepts. Any specific realm of knowledge reflects larger intellectual developments, and ancient geography is no exception. Some specific examples are the emerging theory of a round rather than a flat earth; new understandings of the relationship between dry land and the sea; and approaches to ethno-geography that emphasized the relationship between climate and character.

Human dimension. Unlike modern geographers, who are interested in all parts of the globe, the ancients investigated only inhabited lands. Uninhabited or desert regions were not surveyed or documented, so that they fell outside the framework of the known world. Continents other than Europe, Asia and Africa were not sought out, and in known lands the extent of knowledge grew only as a result of demographic growth and military conquest.[5] Some attempts were made to explore unknown areas, and natural curiosity inflamed imagination. But, generally speaking, regions at the edge of the known world were considered not only dangerous and frightening but irrelevant, as empty land without human inhabitants. Thus the Greeks after Herodotus, and later the Romans, referred to the world as an *oikoumenê* ('inhabited', modifying an implied *gê*), denoting its human aspect as a place of habitation (*oikia*) and excluding

---

[4] On geography in other pre-modern societies, see Raaflaub and Talbert (2010).
[5] Cary (1949).

uninhabited portions, hypothetical landmasses and the ocean deemed to sur-round the *oikoumenê*.

Technique. Modern geography relies on aerial photography (roughly since the First World War), satellite imagery and geographical information systems (GIS), and emphasizes precise quantitative methodology conveyed through maps and statistics.[6] The Greeks and Romans relied primarily on sensory impressions and logical argumentation, and occasionally conveyed their understandings in elaborate verbal reports. Their methods and instruments were simple,[7] but this did not prevent them from achieving impressive scientific breakthroughs. The history of ancient geography is thus, in part, a survey of scientific methodologies, showing how elaborate calculations were carried out using primitive tools.

The study of geographical concepts and practices in antiquity is important for several reasons. The simplest is the linguistic and toponymic contribution of antiquity to modern terminology: the terms 'Europe', 'Atlantic' and 'climate', for example, all have Greek origins. More important, the ancients supplied the foundations for modern science in general, and for modern geography in particular. By raising questions for the first time, and by analysing problems and supplying calculations and taxonomies, they dealt with themes that still occupy geographers today. Despite the simplicity of their tools, the Greeks and the Romans attempted to explore their world, to measure it and understand its natural and human phenomena. At the same time, it is rewarding simply to examine how geographical notions functioned in pre-modern societies, and to consider what specific interests and activities classical geography involved.

This introductory chapter introduces two general themes, independent of any specific time, place or genre, but essential to the understanding of ancient geography. The first (1.3) is how geographical discussions, the development of genres and the progress of knowledge relate to territorial expansion and conquest in different periods, or, put another way, the nature of the connection between the politics of expansion and geographical knowledge and awareness. This issue is closely related to the second theme (1.4): a comparison of Greek and Roman geography. It is generally held that in the cultural and intellectual realms, Rome followed Greece. But was this also the situation in regard to geography?

This book inevitably mentions many specific names, authors and works. It is nonetheless beyond its scope to discuss all the relevant evidence. Our goal is instead to offer, to the extent that is possible, a

---

[6] Cosgrove (2008).   [7] Lewis (2001); Cuomo (2007).

coherent panoramic view of our topic, and to highlight major trends and directions within it.

That any investigation of Greek and Roman society depends on limited sources is well known. However, while some issues can be illuminated by reference to both written sources and archaeological findings, the study of classical geography, including cartography (though there are hardly any original remains of ancient maps), relies mostly on written documentation, including inscriptions. In addition, as noted above, the particular development of the field, and the fact that geography was directly connected to social and political experience, meant that there was no separated, defined geographical genre, and that geographical information appeared in different literary styles and contexts.

Throughout antiquity, a variety of designations and titles were attached to written works that dealt with geographical issues. Specific denominations generally reflected content and structure but there was no standard terminology. As we shall see, the ancients themselves sometimes confused titles and formats, but this should not prevent us from attempting to define some basic terminology attached to written geographical records. What follows is a brief outline of genres and literary formats associated with classical geography, presented in an order intended to reflect a gradation in the amount of detail: from basic, minimal lists to elaborate, lengthy descriptions.

Periploi.[8] Greek civilization began in the Aegean, and for demographic and economic reasons spread to the western coasts of Asia Minor, to Sicily and southern Italy, further west and south to southern France, south-east Spain and North Africa, and all around the Black Sea. Sea routes and seafaring were central to daily life, and were essential for commerce and for voyages of exploration. For the sake of safety and better orientation, navigation was usually restricted to routes along coastlines. This habit became the basis for a genre of written reports known as *periploi* (sing. *periplous*, 'sailing around, circumnavigation'). These records typically presented practical information about sites situated on maritime routes, usually along coasts or rivers, arranged according to the order of a journey along a coastline, including harbour names, distances between sites (often defined according to the number of sailing days), directions and basic local information. To these bare details, more information was sometimes added, for example information about local topography, history and ethnography. They

[8] Janni (1984); Dilke (1985), 130–144; Prontera (1992); Burian (2007).

included occasional references to the interior that could be more extended than merely cataloguing sailing possibilities along navigable rivers. Records of the contours of islands normally came at the end of such surveys. This practical data, spread at first through word of mouth shared by experienced navigators, was converted into written form to help future travellers, mainly colonizers and tradesmen. What sprang first from records of actual travellers' tales became the organizational principle for texts not based on such trips. Gradually *periploi* gained a descriptive dimension through the inclusion of references to man-made monuments, flora and fauna, and ethnographic detail (2.3).

Itineraria.[9] Like Greek *periploi*, the organizational style of which was derived from the linear order supplied by voyages along coastlines, the Latin *itinerarium* (from *iter* 'journey, march') supplied travellers – including troops of soldiers – with catalogued information about stations and distances along Roman routes. The massive expansion of the Roman state by the end of the Republic, and especially from the Augustan age on, required administrative adjustments allowing emissaries of the centre of power in Rome easy access to remote parts of the Empire. With this end in mind, the Romans established an elaborate and efficient road system (the *cursus publicus*), first in Italy and then in various parts of Europe, Asia and the Near East.[10] This road network became the linear basis for some Roman *itineraria* and later for Christian pilgrimage records (2.3).

Periêgêsis and *periodos gês*. Interest in inland regions emerged particularly in the Hellenistic period, as a result of the wider scope of travel and growing curiosity about new countries and peoples. Exhaustive geographical surveys incorporating references to such regions, later defined as *periêgêseis* ('guided tours around'), consisted of far more than mere lists. Instead, they offered surveys in prose or verse of landscapes, topographies, flora and fauna, and details about local inhabitants, their appearance and their habits. A closely related term for such surveys was *periodos* ('going around'), in the sense of a description of a journey. The word most commonly appears in the expression *periodos gês*, used for a description of the entire world rather than a particular region within it.

Chôrographia. Detailed descriptions of narrower regions or specific countries emerged mostly in the Hellenistic age. The common term for such surveys was *chôrographia*, referring to a description of a *chôra* ('country, region'), as opposed to a *geôgraphia* (i.e. a description of the entire earth).[11] Works such as *Persika* (Ctesias) and *Indika* (Ctesias and Megasthenes) belong to this category. But the term *chôrographia* can also be used to refer to the description of a particular region within the wider context of a universal geography, for example as in the case of the regional surveys in individual books of Strabo's *Geography* (2.1).

---

[9] Brodersen (2001), esp. 12–14; Salway (2001), esp. 32–43; Brodersen (2003), 165–190.
[10] Casson (1974), 163–175; Kolb (2001).
[11] See definitions in Strabo 2.5.13 and Ptolemy, *Geog.* 1.1, which imply a difference also in scope and in detail. This might explain the definition of Pomponius Mela's work on the entire inhabited world – supposedly a *periodos gês* – as a *chôrographia*.

Topographical and ethnographical information was also offered in digressions or excurses from the main chronological and narrative line in historical works and the like.[12] The primary focus of such works, of course, was political and military events and the individuals who participated in them. But to assess such events, and especially strategic manoeuvres, often required familiarity with the spatial and human circumstances of the scene. The need for locations, topographies, toponyms and distances thus meant that geographical discussion became fundamental to historiography and related genres. Herodotus set the standard by including in his *Histories* extended descriptions of regions under Persian domination such as Egypt, India and Scythia. Such apparent digressions became an important feature of later historical surveys, for example, those by Thucydides, Polybius, Sallust and Tacitus. Such geographical excurses often adopted the laconic style of early *periploi* and *periodoi*, although their natures also reflected individual authors' personalities and tastes. Because geographical excurses played a crucial role in advancing the narrative line, they were often essential and integral to the enterprise. This topic is explored in detail in 2.2.

Modern scholars have attempted to define an ancient geographical prose genre. Felix Jacoby believed that all ancient prose texts had a single literary foundation, from which sub-genres emerged in an evolutionary fashion. Jacoby defined historiography broadly as a literary style that included all forms of non-fictional prose, suggesting that the contents and organizational principles of historiographic and geographical works were very similar.[13] A traditional, narrower approach sees historiography and geography as separate entities, the one acting as a background for the other.[14] On this analysis, geographical and ethnographical sections within historiographic works were mere digressions with no integral connection to the main narrative. No significant differences in the grammatical constructions and vocabulary of historiographies, of their geographical 'digressions' and of independent works devoted to descriptive geography, are apparent. Therefore the broader context of such 'digressions', as well as the purpose of the author, must also be considered separately for each work. Does the geographical issue feature a mere stylistic variation of the main line of narrative? Could this 'geography' be deleted without affecting the main text's meaning? To what extent is an individual digression

---

[12] Pothou (2009), esp. 19–27, 49–71.
[13] Schepens (1997), and, most important, Clarke (1999), 1–77.
[14] For a list of works that fall somewhere between historiography and geography, see Prontera (1984), 198–199.

an integral and necessary part of the whole? Answers to such questions must be sought in each work individually. Finally, brief mention must be made of sections of classical literature that are 'geographical' neither in goals nor in central subject matter, but that still include geographical thought and information. A 'geographical reading'[15] thus calls attention, for example, to numerous scattered passages in Greek tragedy and comedy, and in Roman epic (2.1).

As will be argued below, there were many styles and contexts for the transmission of geographical issues in the writings of antiquity. No rules or consensus seem to have existed, and even if later authors occasionally criticized their predecessors, a wide choice of formats was available for transmitting knowledge and ideas. This is clear from Strabo's announcement of his intention of describing Greece:

This subject was first treated by Homer; and then, after him, by several others, some of whom have written special treatises entitled *Harbours* or *Periploi* or *Periodoi gês* or the like; and in these is comprised also the description of Greece. Others have set forth the topography of the continents in separate parts of their general histories, for instance, Ephorus and Polybius. Still others have inserted certain things on this subject in their treatises on physics and mathematics, for instance, Posidonius and Hipparchus. (Strabo 8.1.1)

The various styles and themes related to geography may also be divided according to their channels of transmission from antiquity to the present. There is some material evidence, for example, the ethnographic personifications in the Sebasteion in Aphrodisias (modern Turkey),[16] as well as epigraphic remains, whether a five-word inscription on a milestone or a monumental list of toponyms and distances such as the *Stadiasmus Lyciae* (p. 116). There is also a relatively large body of intact texts, as well as papyri preserving fragments of others. Last but not least, many 'geographical' fragments are preserved in collections of the remains of 'lost' Greek and Roman historians and tragic and comic poets.[17] Finally, we

---

[15] Nicolet (1991), 8. [16] Smith (1988).

[17] The two collections specifically focused on geography are Carl Müller's *Geographi Graeci Minores* (*GGM*) (1855–1861) and Alexander Riese's *Geographi Latini Minores* (*GLM*) (1878), while Aubrey Diller (1952) offered an additional treatment of 'minor' Greek geographers. The 'minor' status of the latter refers to the number and size of preserved excerpts; in fact, some of them, such as Hipparchus and Eratosthenes, were important path-breakers and central sources for later geographers. Several new projects to collect geographical fragments are under way: *FGrHist* v, under the supervision of the Deutsches Archäologisches Institut; Budé, *Les géographes grecs*, for which see Marcotte (2002); Graham Shipley's *Selected Greek Geographers* (*SGG*), for which see Shipley (2007); and individual studies, e.g. Marcotte (1990); Brodersen (1994a); Cappelletto (2003); Korenjak (2003).

owe some knowledge to medieval transmission of texts in both prose and verse, and of images, for example, later reconstructions of Ptolemy and the Peutinger Map.

1.3 GEOGRAPHY AND POLITICS

Ancient affairs of state had a close relationship with geography.[18] Military campaigns were often stimulated by expanding geographical horizons, and ideally required well-established geographical information to succeed. At the same time, political achievements and military conquests enhanced geographical knowledge and expanded the borders of the known world both physically and conceptually. It is therefore no coincidence that the history of geography in antiquity is often associated with conquest. Generally speaking, geography and politics nourished one another.

The first systematic Greek description of countries and nations emerged in the fifth century BCE, from Herodotus' desire to describe the extent of the Persian Empire. This enormous kingdom amazed him and, because it included remote regions and – from a Greek point of view – unknown peoples, the project of describing it raised for the first time the need to arrange information systematically on Indians, Scythians, Egyptians, Ethiopians and their countries. The link between political expansion and geographical knowledge is apparent, for example, in Herodotus' account of Darius' project to track the course of the Indus river (4.44). By sending Scylax of Caryanda to sail down the river, the king learned about the 30-month journey by this route across the Indian Ocean into the Red Sea and up to Egypt. He then conquered India and its sea. In addition, Darius' initiative to improve the road system throughout the Persian Empire made travel easy for his officials, but also for other travellers such as Herodotus and later authors who included geographical information in their accounts (on these royal roads see 5.1).

Another significant non-Greek political power was Carthage, which controlled the sea-routes in the western Mediterranean. Carthage's contribution to classical geography is important, because the Greeks admired Carthaginian achievements and transmitted their records, which were translated into Greek at an early stage (chapter 2). According to tradition, around 500 BCE Hanno of Carthage sailed with a large expedition from Carthage (modern Tunis) through the Straits of Gibraltar and down the African coast, reaching the regions facing the Canary Islands

[18] Cary (1949).

and founding Carthaginian colonies along the way. His contemporary Himilco attempted a similar outer-sea adventure, but sailed toward the north, off the shores of Europe. The same pattern is apparent here: a combination of ability, need and curiosity drove economic and military powers to increase their geographic knowledge in the hope of material gain, particularly commodities and land.

Within the Greek world, the first sign of a correlation between politics and geography appears when interests beyond local *poleis* emerged. The Athenians, leading a league of allies officially formed to continue confronting the Persians after the Battle of Mycale in 479 BCE, founded a number of settlements and garrisons in the Aegean region. Athens did not choose these sites by chance. Even when the official pretext was local strife or the suspicious behaviour of the indigenous population, the choice of sites was revealing from a geo-political point of view: Scyros (476 BCE), an island in the centre of the Aegean Sea; Carystus (472 BCE), a *polis* on the southern tip of Euboea facing Attica and the Aegean; Naxos (*c.* 468 BCE), an island in the southern Aegean; and Thasos (463 BCE), an island in the northern Aegean. All these points were important strategically and facilitated control of the Aegean region. There can be little doubt that the Athenians and their leaders had an itinerary of the stages used in shipping, which made them aware of the strategic benefits of holding these points.[19]

But this is perhaps not surprising: these geographical advances may be attributed to the by then long-established acquaintance of Athenian mariners with the Aegean. The colonial horizons of the Archaic period and the commercial ventures of the Greeks had long ago turned the Aegean into the extended 'back yard' of central Greece. Moreover, archaeological evidence of early sanctuaries indicates that the new Athenian settlements and garrisons were founded in places that offered access to economic and particularly agricultural resources and hospitable coasts, forming a 'religious space' reflecting early geographical knowledge.[20] The scope of the geographical knowledge of mainland Greeks thus probably included the Aegean and the Cycladic islands, Crete and the western coasts of Asia Minor. At the same time, there are hints of the limits of geographical horizons and of a lack of knowledge of regions beyond the bounds of the Aegean. Thucydides (6.1.2; 7.44), for example, indicates that most

[19] Constantakopoulou (2007). See also the promotion of an imperialistic ideology through geographical means in Aeschylus' *Eumenides*: Futo Kennedy (2006).
[20] De Polignac (1995); Boardman (1999).

ordinary Athenians were not acquainted with the topography of Sicily and therefore miscalculated when they decided to invade the island. These instances prove that by the fifth century BCE, geographical knowledge was still limited in scope, and in some cases this ignorance affected political decisions.

In the decades after the Peloponnesian War, which concluded with the end of Athenian domination of the Greek regions of the Mediterranean, geographical data and ideas continued to feature in works of various scholars such as Aristotle, Ephorus and Timaeus. In these years, until the emergence of Macedonian rule, there was no solid hegemony in the Greek world and the mutual relationship between political drives and geographical ideas was less conspicuous. Geographical discussions, however, were not neglected.

But then the campaigns of Alexander produced one of the most obvious demonstrations in world history of the relationship between geography and politics. Under Alexander, there was not only territorial expansion on an unprecedented scale, but also for the first time a deliberate, active search for new horizons. While the aspirations of Alexander's father Philip II, to the extent they can be assessed, seem to have been limited to neighbouring lands, Alexander cast his gaze toward remote horizons even when these seemed fantastic. It is difficult to separate fact from fiction in Alexander's story, because the king's later achievements stimulated the invention of a character with strong mythic overtones. But there can be no doubt that Alexander's ventures were closely tied up with geographical investigation. He reached remote points, some of which had not been visited by Greeks before his time, except perhaps sporadically by individuals. Some ancient sources even offered the image of a king who combined a desire for political power with scientific interests, representing him as someone wishing to watch and learn, not only to conquer, and ordering his men to record the details of unknown regions.[21] Be that as it may, these records turned into an impressive body of evidence – even if occasionally exaggerated – on human habits, flora and fauna, topography and climate.

Both in Alexander's lifetime and after it, the story of his achievements was expanded and exaggerated by geographical means. It was already known in antiquity, for example, that sites had been 'moved' to create a greater impact:

---

[21] But see the reservations expressed by Romm (1989b), and the discussion below.

Not everybody accepts the glorifying stories, and their fabricators were men who thought about flattery rather than about truth. For instance, they transferred the Caucasus to the region of the Indian mountains. (Strabo 11.5.5)

Geography had been politically recruited to contribute to the king's magnificent image.

When Alexander reached the upper Indus river (in modern Pakistan), his troops refused to proceed further east: they were tired and could see no clear destination. The extent to which Alexander himself knew where he was going is difficult to tell. The king was apparently driven by an intense urge to march toward the unknown limits of the *oikoumenē*, and was perhaps inspired by the legendary travels of Heracles, who was supposedly his ancestor, and by those of the Assyrian queen Semiramis.[22]

A few decades later, the growth of the Roman state, starting with the territorial and political achievements of the Punic Wars against Carthage, put Rome literally on the map of world powers. The annexation of Sicily at the end of the First Punic War (241 BCE) extended Roman power beyond the Italian peninsula and (as in the case of other empires, both earlier and later) 'appetite came with eating'.[23] This growth relied also on the Roman tendency to absorb cultural elements of the Hellenistic world, including an intellectual interest in geography.[24] Rome soon became the ruler of all regions around the Mediterranean, which came to be described as 'our sea' (*mare nostrum*; e.g. Plin. *Nat.* 6.142).[25]

This rapid and unprecedented phenomenon required an explanation, and several ancient scholars, mostly Greeks, attempted to offer one. Polybius, who witnessed Roman expansion in the earlier second century BCE, claimed that Rome's mixed constitution and efficient army were the basis for its power.[26] About 150 years later, when the Roman Empire under Augustus was larger than ever, Strabo offered a geographical explanation: Rome dominated the world because it was located at its centre, and the city's natural features made it fit to rule.[27] Geographical advantages and political power were thus directly connected.

Although modern interpretations of the motivations behind Roman expansion differ, it is clear that, as the Republic grew more dependent

[22] Sulimani (2005).
[23] After François Rabelais, *Gargantua*, chapter 5 (1542); see F. Gray's edition (Paris, 1995), 72.
[24] Momigliano (1975).
[25] Burr (1932). On the significance and role of the Mediterranean, see Cary (1949), 1–36; Horden and Purcell (2000); Abulafia (2011).
[26] Polyb. 6.11–42. For similar notions connecting Rome's vast conquests with its military excellence, see Vegetius, *De re militari* 1.1.
[27] Strabo, 6.4.1 and similarly Vitruvius, *De architectura*, 6.1.11.

on individual politicians, their personal ambitions to conquer the world played a significant role in the growth of the city's power. In this age of territorial expansion, the geographical significance of conquest was expressed in geographical *cognomina* (surnames).[28] A group of Latin *cognomina* was derived from geographical terms, mostly peoples, tribes, regions and towns, and, to a lesser extent, mountains and rivers. As early as the sixth century BCE, the *cognomina* of the Roman nobility recorded the places of origin of their bearers, and at this stage there were no examples of foreign ethnics. From the third century BCE, however, when conquests became significant, *cognomina* derived from conquered towns and peoples are attested, although only among the nobility. These were honorary *cognomina* conferred on victors, e.g. Africanus, Asiaticus, Macedonicus, Ponticus and Balearicus. The geographical significance of conquests thus encouraged further expansion, by contributing to the political reputation of individual magistrates.

Pompey, Julius Caesar and Augustus, each in his own way, aspired to conquer regions never reached before.[29] The idea of Rome as a dominant world power was often expressed in literature depicting the Roman state as the ruler of the entire *orbis terrarum* and as conqueror of all nations.[30] At the same time, individual leaders aspired to extend the territory of the state, along with their own reputation. Their ambitions were derived almost consciously from the mythical conquests of Alexander.[31] Thus Pompey's campaigns in the east are depicted in the sources with unprecedented and even exaggerated terminology emphasizing his extraordinary geographical achievements:

Inscriptions borne in advance of the procession indicated the nations over which [Pompey] triumphed. These were: Pontus, Armenia, Cappadocia, Paphlagonia, Media, Colchis, Iberia, Albania, Syria, Cilicia, Mesopotamia, Phoenicia and Palestine, Judaea, Arabia … and cities not much under nine hundred in number, besides eight hundred pirate ships, while thirty-nine cities had been founded … But that which most enhanced his glory and had never been the achievement of any Roman before, was that he celebrated his third triumph over the third continent. For others before him had celebrated three triumphs; but he celebrated his first over Libya (Africa), his second over Europe, and this his last over Asia, so that he seemed in a way to have included the whole world in his three triumphs. (Plutarch, *Pompey*, 45)[32]

---

[28] Kajanto (1965), 43–53.   [29] Brunt (1978); Nicolet (1991).
[30] Cicero, *Philippics*, 4.14–15; *For Murena*, 22.
[31] Michel (1967); Weippert (1972).   [32] See Östenberg (2009).

Julius Caesar also aspired to open up new horizons for the Romans, as is apparent from his account of his campaigns in Gaul. Augustus expressly acknowledged the same idea in his record of his achievements, the *Res Gestae* (sections 25–33), claiming, for example:

> I extended the borders of all the provinces of the Roman People which neighboured nations not subject to our rule … I sailed my ships on the Ocean from the mouth of the Rhine to the eastern region up to the borders of the Cimbri, where no Roman had gone before that time by land or sea. (section 26)

The emperors after Augustus embraced similar ideas. After his campaign in Britain in 43 CE, Claudius (surnamed 'Britannicus') 'set a naval crown on the gable of the Palace beside the civic crown as a sign that he had crossed and, as it were, subdued the Ocean' (Suet. *Claud.* 17), while Trajan ('Dacicus') celebrated his victories over Dacia (101–106 CE) by erecting a monumental column in the Roman Forum depicting his campaigns. Such sentiments had been summed up already in the first century BCE in Dionysius of Halicarnassus' excited comment:

> Rome rules every country that is not inaccessible or uninhabited, and she is mistress of every sea, not only of that which lies inside the Pillars of Heracles but also of the Ocean, except that part of it which is not navigable. She is the first and the only state recorded in all time that ever made the risings and the settings of the sun the boundaries of her dominion … she was emboldened to aspire to govern all mankind … she no longer had as rival any nation either barbarian or Greek … and there is no nation … that disputes or protests against being ruled by her universal dominion. (*Roman Antiquities*, 1.3.3, 5)

These vast conquests, together with the pacification of hostile nations and eradication of piracy (*Pax Romana*), produced a large empire whose borders overlapped with the boundaries of the *oikoumenê*.[33] This geo-political reality was further harnessed to promote political goals. Roman poets, particularly in the Augustan period, took great pride and joy in enumerating subdued nations and strange new toponyms. In this way they expressed their delight in the growing and strengthening Empire, which was directly associated with the character of the *princeps*, while geographical names had an emotional effect on the audience.[34] Moreover, geographical vocabulary played a part in visual public discourse: personified images of conquered nations on monuments such as triumphal arches and coins and engraved lists of regions and tribes all reflected imperial

---

[33] On the Roman concept and practice of setting borders, see Wheeler (1954); Isaac (1992); Braund (1996); Whittaker (2000); Talbert (2005).
[34] Mayer (1986); Grant (2000).

achievements and promoted the prestige of individual men as well as the glory and pride of the Roman people.

In antiquity, political achievements seem to have been assessed in terms of territorial expansion and not of head-counts of subdued populations. Praise was awarded for the expansion of physical borders, especially for the conquest of inhabited or fertile land that could support agriculture and human habitation. Even when names of nations and tribes were mentioned, they seem to have represented physical regions. Augustus, in his *Res Gestae*, and other Roman leaders did not boast about the number of conquered persons but, if they were mentioned at all, about the captives' rank: the higher it was, the more magnificent the achievement. Remote nations and especially those who inhabited the edges of the world (Indians, Britons, Scythians) counted as particularly valuable acquisitions. Exotic and strange names, habits and natural phenomena enhanced the atmosphere of extraordinary achievement.

In conclusion: once geographical horizons are extended, curiosity is both satisfied and aroused. This driving force, particularly in warlike societies tending toward political and territorial expansion, becomes an engine for the extension of power: knowledge of a region creates the will to conquer it, and conquest of a region enhances knowledge. 'Knowledge is power',[35] in a practical sense, as geographical knowledge facilitates military victory and conquest, but also intellectually: geographical knowledge creates powerful rulers as it is exploited for propaganda purposes, contributing to the further expansion of power.

1.4 GREEK AND ROMAN GEOGRAPHY

Geography engaged Greek and Roman authors of various social, intellectual and political statuses. Generally, these men were all both highly educated and curious, but there was a clear difference between, for example, Aristotle as a Greek scientist, Scylax of Caryanda as a Hellenized Carian traveller, Julius Caesar as a Roman conqueror, and Pomponius Mela as a Roman scholar. The distinction is not merely a matter of whether these authors wrote in Greek or Latin, and the question of the extent of the difference (if any) between Greek and Roman geography nonetheless arises. An answer to, or at least an elucidation of, the question may be sought in the social and political contexts of geographical interest

---

[35] Francis Bacon, *Meditationes Sacrae De Haeresibus* (1597).

in Greek and Roman society, with the *caveat* that both societies went through different periods and phases. Although oversimplification should be avoided, some general tendencies are apparent.

Rome consciously and deliberately adopted some basic components of Greek culture, such as literature and art, and assumed Greek precedents when imitating Greek achievements. In this sense, geography was no exception: the Romans adopted Greek traditions both stylistically and conceptually. Strabo comments that Roman authors generally are 'imitators of the Greeks' and that 'what they relate they merely translate from the Greeks' (3.4.19). The history of classical geography doubtless begins with Greek geography and is dominated by Greek authors for several centuries. But were the Romans merely keepers of literary and conceptual traditions? Key to the answer to that question are the different political and social circumstances in the two cultures, which influenced their worldviews. Generally speaking, the changing paradigm of a smaller world based on local maritime communities, as opposed to a larger land-empire, determined how geography was grasped and functioned. It also seems self-evident that geography in an imperial context seeks and describes different matters than it did in the Archaic colonization period or during the campaigns of Alexander.

Greeks aspired to document sea-routes and extend coastal horizons for primarily mercantile purposes. The main channels for the acquisition of new geographical information were explorations by traders, often sponsored by non-Greek kings and rulers: Egyptians (Necho sponsoring the Phoenicians), Carthaginians (Hanno and Himilco), or Persians (Darius I sponsoring Scylax of Caryanda). But sheer intellectual inquisitiveness also formed the basis for some scientific quests, which were typically Greek (starting with the Presocratic philosophers). Astronomical calculations and mathematical conclusions pertaining to geography were accordingly almost exclusively the product of Greek genius, and were then imitated and transmitted by later Roman authors.

Rome for its part promoted the association of geography and war. On the assumptions that topography influenced strategy, and that geographical knowledge affected successful warfare, the Romans nurtured geographical documentation to improve their own physical orientation in the field.[36] Greek historians (Herodotus, Thucydides, Polybius) had already

---

[36] Isaac (1996); Elton (2004) *pace* Syme (1988), who claims that defeat did not result from geographical ignorance but from other factors, such as harsh topography, over-confidence or treason. But

realized the need to include relevant geographical detail in their accounts to explain battlefield tactics and help educate future military leaders. The same pattern prevailed in Roman historiography, for instance in Sallust. But the Romans, with their emphasis on practicality, improved this tendency by replacing academic, *post factum* analysis with on-the-ground assessment, as in Caesar's *Gallic War*. There are hints at an earlier interest of both Cornelius Nepos and Cicero in composing more theoretical geographical treatises involving measurements and descriptions of various regions in the world.[37] Nepos' work was apparently not widely disseminated, however, while Cicero abandoned his project for fear of Greek criticism. What did survive of Roman interest in geographical issues demonstrates that the Romans were far less interested in pure science, and acquired new geographical information mainly from military conquests. They used very simple maps, and they were satisfied with mere *itineraria* to discover locations and distances.

The use of geography for political promotion also requires consideration. As was noted above, geography played a significant role in Roman imperial circles, reflecting Roman aspirations and achievements. Indeed, some important geographical works written in Greek (for instance those of Strabo, Dionysius 'Periegetes' and Ptolemy) are so imbued with Roman political orientation that classifying them as 'Greek geographies' is almost meaningless.

To sum up, the relationship between practical needs and literary geography determined the degree of interest in both societies, but there is no clear-cut way to assess the 'Greekness' or 'Romanness' of ancient works related to geography, and many 'neutral' texts have no specific temporal or political pertinence. Perhaps it could be cautiously said, however, that the Greeks, at least in the earlier periods, were often interested in coasts (including those outside the Mediterranean), the western parts of the Mediterranean and sea-routes in general, whereas the Romans were more interested in hinterland regions, frontier territories and countries at the edge of the known world, particularly in northern Europe and eastern Asia. The questions the cultures asked were also different. The Greeks wanted to know about the size and shape of countries, as well as details of travel routes, local commodities and the traits of the inhabitants of different places. The Romans

most conquered lands were previously unknown to the Romans and required intelligence gathered in the field; see Austin and Rankov (1995); Bertrand (1997).
[37] Nepos: Geiger (1985), 76–77; Cicero: *Att.* 2.6.1.

tended to look for information about distances, topographies and foreign nations, details that contributed to a better physical orientation.
Finally, geography seems to have served slightly different, even if not
entirely dichotomous, goals for each group: for the Greeks maritime
navigation aimed primarily at commerce and scientific investigation,
whereas for the Romans land-routes fulfilled chiefly administrative
and military purposes.[38]

---

[38] This is not to say, of course, that there were no Greek land expeditions and topographical intelligence and no Roman commercial journeys by sea.

CHAPTER 2

Descriptive geography

2.1 EPIC, MYTH AND POETRY

The prehistoric clay tablets inscribed in Linear B script and archaeological evidence expose the nature of geographical perception in Mycenaean culture.[1] The 'Pylian geography' from the south-western Peloponnese included lists of toponyms arranged from north to south, showing that the Mycenaeans utilized a number of basic spatial concepts and could conceive of a systematic, consistent conceptualization of their surroundings. A more solid starting-point for the history of ancient geography, however, as the ancients themselves realized, is the earliest literary evidence from the Greek world: the Homeric epics (*c.* 700 BCE).

Geographical issues were by no means reserved for prose compositions: numerous geographical details, concepts and descriptions appear in the Greek and Roman poetic corpora. As the section that follows is designed to demonstrate, early myths, which were at first orally transmitted, were moulded into new poetic patterns while preserving reminiscences of geographical situations from previous generations. These myths are thus important evidence for any discussion of geography in antiquity. Another area of study connected to the ties between poetry and geography is the inspection of the sporadic geographical titbits preserved in poetic genres such as epic and drama. But most important and most curious are poetic compositions – both Greek and Roman – devoted entirely to geographical themes. As will be argued below, even scientific geography used poetic expressions. A general survey of evidence drawn from poetic myths, passing poetic references and surviving complete texts shows that poems in various ages revealed a consistent worldview.

Relying on earlier oral traditions, the *Iliad* and the *Odyssey* preserved ideas of spatial orientation, details of actual land and sea travels, records

[1] Bennet (1999).

of early toponyms, and echoes of ethnographic notions.[2] Because of all this information, the traditional author of the poems, 'Homer', was later dubbed 'the founder of geography' (Strabo 1.1.2), and his geographical concepts and the informative details he offered remained important throughout antiquity, playing a leading role in many geographical discussions.[3]

In addition to allusions to early topographies, ethnographic details and toponyms, several commonplaces in the *Iliad* and the *Odyssey* supply the basis for reconstructing the geographical worldview of the author and his age. The elaborate, lively scene represented by the smith god Hephaestus on the divine shield of Achilles (*Il.* 18.468–617) depicts an encapsulated image of a wide range of human conduct and activities: a wedding, a trial, a battle, agricultural work and dancing.[4] All these take place in two cities situated on dry land and surrounded by the waters of the Ocean depicted on the rim of the shield. Occasional passages in the *Odyssey* (e.g. *Od.* 11.14–19) hint at the same concept of the world as a large round island surrounded by an unlimited 'deep flowing Ocean, from which all rivers flow and all the sea and all springs and deep wells' (*Il.* 21.195–196). The image of dry land surrounded by Ocean also appeared about the same time in the pseudo-Hesiodic *Shield of Heracles* (314–317) and persisted throughout antiquity even when the size of the known world grew larger and its actual shape became better known (3.1).[5]

Another Homeric passage of geographical significance, this time preserving local information, is the so-called 'Catalogue of Ships'.[6] In *Iliad* 2.493–877, the poet lists the Achaean forces waging war on Troy by their regional origins, including lists of cities and some epithets containing brief geographical, and specifically topographical, information. He observes that the Boeotians, for example, inhabited among other sites 'rocky Aulis … and mountainous Eteonos … and grassy Haliartos … and they had Arne, rich in grapes … and Anthedon on the edge' (*Il.* 2.494–508). The value of this catalogue lies in the toponyms it preserves and also in how it organizes them into geographical units arranged in a particular order. These details show that the author and the traditions he preserved had an established knowledge of the physical, demographic and political layout of these regions. The verses offer an orderly geographical picture, which

[2] Ballabriga (1986); (1998); Romm (1992), 172–214; Dickie (1995).
[3] Biraschi (2005).
[4] Hardie (1985); Clay (1992), 132–137.
[5] Romm (1992), 11–13.
[6] Hope Simpson and Lazenby (1970); Visser (1997).

supplied later authors, such as Polybius and Strabo, with a framework for arranging their own geographical surveys.[7] The same catalogue also includes toponymic 'fossils', that is, names of cities and regions which were destroyed in later periods, such as Eutresis in Boeotia, Crisa in Phocis, and Dorion and Pylos in Messenia.[8] Because of the geographical (topographic and ethnographic) importance of the 'Catalogue', the works of ancient scholars who investigated it, such as Demetrius of Scepsis and Apollodorus of Athens, became significant sources for later geographers such as Strabo.

The geographical horizons of the Homeric age are also apparent in the sections of the poem devoted to the wanderings of Odysseus. The Greek hero makes an adventurous journey from Troy in western Asia Minor to his home on Ithaca in the Ionian Sea. In addition to legendary elements, the plot apparently depicts real scenery and sea-routes. The audience hears of islands such as Zacynthos (*Od.* 9.24) and Cythera (*Od.* 9.81), and may glean an idea of actual nautical orientation through remarks such as 'Menelaus joined us at Lesbos, and found us making up our minds about our course, for we did not know whether to go outside Chios by the island of Psyra, keeping this to our left, or inside Chios, over against the stormy headland of Mimas' (*Od.* 3.168–172). There is in addition an account of Menelaus' journey home after the war, when his ship was blown off course to Egypt. When Menelaus sums up his seven-year-long adventure, he says: 'I roamed past Cyprus and Phoenicia and Egypt and came to Ethiopians, Erembrians, and to Libya' (*Od.* 4.81–85). This report puzzled ancient scholars, some of whom suggested that Menelaus made a coasting voyage (*periplous*) along the African coast, perhaps sailing around the entire continent and even reaching India (Strabo 1.2.31).

The Homeric epics can thus be used to assess the general limits of geographical knowledge, beyond which mythic notions took over. Actual geography eventually gave way to myth, and one can almost mentally map the zones where solid information becomes vague. The real geographical framework of the Homeric epics seems to include the following regions: mainland Greece, the Aegean islands, the western coast of Asia Minor, Crete and Egypt. To the wider mythic framework belong Ethiopia, the Black Sea region, and part of the western Mediterranean. The world of the epics is thus relatively narrow.

---

[7] Polybius in Book 34, and Strabo mainly in Books 8–10 on Greece.
[8] Hope Simpson and Lazenby (1970), 153–154.

A similar borderline between real and mythic geography can be detected in other poetic corpora. Like the Homeric epics, Hesiod's *Theogony* and *Works and Days* preserve geographical notions, despite most likely having no intention of dealing directly with geographical themes.[9] Hesiod thus expressed the concept of the surrounding Ocean by hinting at the connection between it and the edge of the world (*Works and Days* 167–171), and enumerated various rivers, as well as Europe and Asia, among Ocean's descendants (*Theogony* 357–359). Another early epic, the *Arimaspea* of Aristeas of Proconnesus, mixed geographical ideas with mythical components, based on the travels of its author.[10] Herodotus 4.13.6 supplies the details:

> There is also a story related in a poem by Aristeas … being then possessed by Phoebus, [he] visited the Issedonians. Beyond these, he said, dwell the one-eyed Arimaspians, beyond whom are the griffins that guard gold, and beyond these again the Hyperboreans, whose territory reaches to the sea … as for the land on which my history has begun to speak, no one exactly knows what lies northward of it. For I can learn from none who claims to know as an eyewitness. Even Aristeas, of whom I lately made mention, even he did not claim to have gone beyond the Issedonians, not even in his poems; but he spoke of what lay northward by hearsay, saying what the Issedonians had told him.

Apparently around 675 BCE, Aristeas travelled north of the Black Sea, beyond the Scythians, and reached the area of the Sea of Azov. Even if we omit discussion of the geographical and ethnographic significance of each detail, the account seems to reflect the actual distribution of habitation in the region, by offering a gradation of population from close to remote, and from real to legendary (the one-eyed Arimaspians and the griffins). The furthest nation mentioned in the report was named after its position beyond Boreas the north wind – hence the name 'Hyperboreans' – and was said to dwell by the outer sea, meaning its furthest northern edge, the Ocean. Aristeas also noted a high mountain range covered in darkness and snow, beyond which the Hyperboreans dwelt. These high peaks were named the Caucasus (in later geographical tradition Rhipaean), and throughout antiquity they marked the northern edge of the earth's land mass (3.1).

The Hyperboreans appear repeatedly in ancient poetry and prose and are depicted as blessed, healthy, happy and just.[11] They accordingly became a utopian symbol for the far north. In this sense they played the same role

---

[9] Clay (1992).   [10] Bolton (1962). Fragments on pp. 207–214.
[11] Hdt. 4.32–36; Pind. *Pyth.* 10.29–46; *Isthm.* 6.23; Romm (1989a); Dillery (1998).

as other mysterious, partially known regions at the edges of the world, such as the Islands of the Blessed, Elysium and Furthest Thule. Diodorus of Sicily 2.47.1–6 offers an elaborate description of the Hyperboreans based on an earlier survey by Hecataeus of Abdera. According to Diodorus, the Hyperboreans inhabit an island about the size of Sicily situated in the Ocean beyond Gaul. On this fertile and temperate island, the moon appears to be particularly close. The inhabitants are friendly, worship Apollo and are ruled by the Boreadae, who are descendants of Boreas. Diodorus also mentions an early Hyperborean named Abaris, who visited Greece and established a friendship with the inhabitants of Delos.

The mixture of myth and fact in early epics is closely connected with the way in which early myths – even if known only from later written versions – preserve morsels of actual facts and concepts, including geographical notions. The following examples serve to illustrate this phenomenon. According to tradition, Prometheus deceived Zeus by tricking him to choose the inedible parts of sacrificial meat, and then stole fire to give it to mankind. For this behaviour, he was punished by being chained to a rock situated at the edge of the world, and his liver was constantly devoured by Zeus' eagle (Hes. *Theog.* 521–531). The physical pain was unbearable, and the penalty also included seclusion from mankind; the remoteness of the rock was thus an essential part of the story. The sources vary as to the exact location of Prometheus' rock, depending on the geographical views and knowledge of each author who engaged with the tradition. Prometheus had to be placed at the edge of the world, but as geographical knowledge increased with time, horizons expanded and the edge of the world moved accordingly. Thus even when Prometheus' rock was placed in the Caucasus Mountains, mentally its geographical location was changed, being placed as far away as India.[12]

Perseus too wandered to the outer limits of the known world. Polydectes, king of Seriphos, sent him to behead Medusa, whose gaze turned all visitors to stone. But before he confronted this danger, Perseus had to locate the abode of Medusa and the other two Gorgons 'who dwell beyond glorious Ocean, in the frontier land towards Night, where are the clear-voiced Hesperides' (Hes. *Theog.* 274–275). In various versions the hero travels to extreme geographical points, or visits characters known to dwell at the edges of the earth: the Hesperidae, the Graeae, Atlas and even the Hyperboreans. This relationship between myth and geography is reflected in later toponymic traditions. Pliny the Elder, for example,

---

[12] Strabo 11.5.5; 15.1.8 and see Finkelberg (1998).

quotes Xenophon of Lampsacus on the topic of the Gorgades Islands, which were two days' sail from the west coast of Africa, and 'formerly the home of the Gorgons' (*HN* 6.200).[13]

The myth of Heracles also featured visits to many places, including the edges of the world. To atone for the murder of his children, Heracles had to fulfil 12 tasks (labours) imposed by his enemy and rival for the Argive throne, Eurystheus. Six labours took place in the Peloponnese: at Nemea (the lion), Lerna (the Hydra), Mount Ceryneia (the hind), Mount Erymanthus (the boar), Elis (Augeas' stables), and Lake Stymphalus in Arcadia (the Stymphalian birds). Two others were performed in Crete (the bull) and in Thrace (Diomedes' mares), and one in the underworld (Cerberus). Heracles' other three labours took him to the edges of the world as they were conceived of at the time the myth was formed. First he had to steal the girdle of Hippolyte, queen of the Amazons. This tribe of female warriors represented in mythology a group of outsiders, in both their cultural norms and their geographical situation,[14] who were placed in various locations on all three continents, but always at the edges of the earth: beyond Troy and in Thrace (*Il.* 3.186–189; 6.186); in Scythia or Sarmatia (Hdt. 4.110); in Themiscyra near the river Thermodon (Aesch. *PV* 723–725); in Libya (Diod. Sic. 3.52–55); on the river Tanais (Plin. *HN* 6.19); near the Caspian Gates (Cleitarchus in Strabo 11.5.4); and in the far east or west (Diod. Sic. 3.52–55). It is significant that in Hellenistic tradition Alexander the Great of Macedon was made to meet the queen of the Amazons beyond the river Jaxartes (the modern Syr-Darya, in Kazakhstan) and in this way was depicted through exaggerated geography as a legendary hero.[15]

Next, Heracles had to herd the cattle of Geryon, a monstrous giant who inhabited the western edge of the world on the island Erytheia, which means 'red' after the colour of the sunset. This island, later identified with one of the islands off Gades (modern Cadiz in Spain; Strabo 3.2.11; Mela 3.47), lay at the western edge of the Mediterranean near a site named after Heracles himself: the Pillars of Heracles (later the Straits of Gibraltar; see 3.1). In the same neighbourhood the hero had to collect apples from trees in the garden of the Hesperides ('daughters of Hesperus (the Evening)'). Ancient traditions located these nymphs' abode either near the place where Atlas bore the sky – again on the western African edge of the world

---

[13] Probably the modern Cape Verde Islands.
[14] Hardwick (1990); Blok (1995), esp. 83–104.
[15] Plin. *HN* 6.49; Plut. *Alex.* 46; Stoneman (1994); Baynham (2001).

(the modern Atlas Mountains, in Morocco) – or on a remote island somewhere in the Atlantic Ocean beyond the Pillars. Heracles also made his
way to another edge of the known world when he released Prometheus
from his constant pain by killing Zeus' eagle. Finally, Heracles joined
the voyage of the Argonauts, whose adventures were the centre of another
detailed myth with geographical significance.

Jason, the only surviving descendant of Aison, king of Iolcus, was
ordered by Pelias, his father's half-brother, who claimed the throne, to
fetch the Golden Fleece from Colchis on the far eastern shore of the
Black Sea. Together with a large group of heroes, he sailed on the ship
Argo, navigating long sea-routes through the eastern Mediterranean and
on major European rivers. The most comprehensive surviving version
of these adventures is the *Argonautica* of Apollonius of Rhodes.[16] This
third-century BCE epic is studded with references to an actual nautical
journey and includes numerous descriptions of landscapes and peoples.
In his four-book poem, Apollonius depicts the route to Colchis through
the Aegean Sea into the Black Sea along its southern shore (Books
1–2). This route was well known in Apollonius' time, mainly through
Mediterranean sailing reports (*periploi*, see 2.3), as is apparent from the
poem's terminology:

> Thence going forward they ran past Meliboea,
> escaping a stormy beach and surf-line.
> And in the morning they saw Homole close at hand
> leaning on the sea and skirted it, and not long after
> they were about to pass by the outfall of the river Amyrus.
> From there they beheld Eurymenae and the sea-washed ravines
> of Ossa and Olympus; next they
> reached the slopes of Pallene beyond the headland of Canastra
> running all night with the wind.
> And at dawn before them as they journeyed rose Athos,
> the Thracian mountain, which with its topmost peak overshadows Lemnos
> even as far as Myrine, though it lies as far off as the space
> that a well-trimmed merchant ship would traverse up to midday.
>
> (*Argon.* 1.592–604)

One of the most dramatic scenes in the epic is the Argonauts' encoun-
ter with the clashing rocks (*Argon.* 1.549–604), called the Symplegades
('clashing, striking') in Apollonius' epic and identified with the Cyanean

---

[16] Delage (1930); Pearson (1938); Harder (1994); Piot (2000); Meyer (2008). Cf. Bacon (1931) on the
fifth-century CE Orphic *Argonautica*.

('blue') Rocks at the entrance to the Bosporus (*Argon.* 1.3; 2.770; 4.1003).[17] Legendary elements and geographical reality intersect here as well, offering a poetic way of illustrating the difficulty of passing through the Black Sea straits. Apollonius, however, also inherited existing popular stories of similar sailing dangers, such as the Wandering Rocks (*Planctae*) (*Od.* 12.59–72), and Scylla and Charybdis (*Od.* 12.85–110), which are rationalized elsewhere into rocks (Ov. *Met.* 14.73–74).

Apollonius' Book 4 describes Jason's journey home on a different route: through the Ister (Danube), the Po and the Rhône to the Mediterranean, and then to Crete, stopping also in North Africa and finally reaching Iolcus in Thessaly. This lesser-known route included exotic and fabulous elements reminiscent of Odysseus' adventures in the *Odyssey*. Apollonius' intellectual background – he was the head of the library at Alexandria – afforded him a double inspiration: Homeric antecedents and scientific geography.

The Roman counterpart of Apollonius' epic was the Latin *Argonautica* composed around 80 CE in Rome by Gaius Valerius Flaccus.[18] Clearly influenced by Apollonius, Flaccus offered a glimpse of an updated geography by alluding to toponyms and ethnonyms not mentioned in Apollonius' epic and by mentioning particularly remote points, such as the Indian river Choaspes (5.602), and the people called Alani (6.42) who lived north of the Caspian Sea.

It is apparent, then, that ancient traditions of early myths preserve echoes of contemporary understandings of the geographical character of the world and hints of actual, primarily maritime, journeys. There are several ways of explaining this connection between myths and geographical information. Myths often gained a touch of authenticity by including real geographical data, making them more plausible. From another perspective, attaching the mythic past to particular sites earned newly discovered places respect, while integrating new data into old orders of knowledge.[19] The ordinary person reading or hearing a myth was probably delighted to recognize familiar locations within chronologically and socially remote stories. The Greek landscape was enriched with mythic events, and modern study of early traditions and their variants, even when legendary elements are involved, is important for assembling evidence for the origins of ancient exploration and geographical awareness.

---

[17] Nishimura-Jensen (2000).
[18] Zissos (2008). Earlier, Varro Atacinus had translated Apollonius' *Argonautica* into Latin.
[19] Bickerman (1952); Veyne (1988).

Early myths were presented primarily in poetry. But later, when considerations of orality and memory for the choice of metrical genres were less relevant, some authors still chose poetry for geographical purposes. This phenomenon is different from geographical allusions in traditional poetic corpora, where random geographical details – even if significant – appeared in verse. In such instances, poetry was the main issue, and geographical traces highlighted decoration, served as ornamentation and supplied information only as a by-product.

The nature of poetic geography, which seems unusual from a modern perspective, requires some discussion. An anonymous geographical composition in iambic trimeters written around 100 BCE and dedicated to King Nicomedes III Euergetes of Bithynia, was attributed by ancient scholars to several hypothetical authors.[20] As in the case of other endeavours, both practical and intellectual, there is a hint here of a monarch sponsoring geographical research. The poet reveals that he chose the iambic metre for its brevity and clarity. After some introductory words, including a dedication to the 'most divine king Nicomedes' (line 2), the surviving 980 verses begin with a section on Europe (139–873), followed by one on Asia (874–980). The author identifies his written sources, mainly Ephorus, Timaeus and Eratosthenes (lines 114–127), but also emphasizes his own travel in Greece, Asia Minor, Italy, Sicily, Libya and Carthage (lines 129–136). The first place mentioned in the survey is Mainake (near modern Malaga, in Spain), founded by Massalia, while the last is the area around the river Sangarius (modern Sakarya, Turkey) on the shores of the Black Sea. The closing sections, which probably included the northern coast of Africa, are lost.

At about the same time (*c.* 100–87 BCE), a certain Dionysius son of Calliphon, possibly from Athens, composed a description of Greece in iambic trimeters.[21] The first 23 lines of the poem, dedicated to an unidentified Theophrastus, reveal the author's name in an acrostic. Dionysius relies specifically on Apollodorus of Athens and Artemidorus of Ephesus, and on an otherwise unknown Athenian historian named Philetas. Only 150 verses survive, including a description in the *periplous* tradition of coasts around Greece, the Aegean islands and Crete, indicating distances in both *stadia* and the number of sailing days.

---

[20] Diller (1952), 165–176; Marcotte (1990), 40–44; (2002); Korenjak (2003). For the text itself, see *GGM* 1.196–237.
[21] For the text, see *GGM* 1.238–243; Marcotte (1990).

The general trend of combining poetry with geographical content is apparent in several other first-century BCE texts. Alexander of Ephesus (75–45 BCE), nicknamed 'Lychnos' ('lamp'), 'left epics in which he arranges the heavenly bodies and describes the continents geographically, dedicating to each continent a poem' (Strabo 14.1.27).[22] Other sources show that Alexander referred to three continents, which hints at a three-part poem. The choice of specific poetic genre was apparently flexible. Geographical content was combined with poetic form by Latin authors as well. Varro Atacinus (82–30 BCE) composed (among other works, including a translation into Latin of Apollonius' *Argonautica*) a didactic *Chorographia* in three books.[23] In this he described the three continents, emphasizing coastlines and flora. He also used astronomy to fix exact locations and offer explanations of climate.

In the second century CE, Dionysius of Alexandria served as director of the imperial libraries in Rome under Hadrian, and as a secretary in charge of imperial correspondence and embassies. Dionysius composed a poetic description of the world in 1,187 hexameter verses, based mainly on Eratosthenes, but also borrowing sections from the earlier poem of Alexander 'Lychnos'.[24] He also gave his own name and a dedication to Hadrian in acrostics. The work, which describes the entire world, including the three continents and the Ocean, earned Dionysius the nickname 'Periegêtês', that is 'author of a *periêgêsis*'. A sample of the poem referring to Asia illustrates the combination of accurate geographical information (shapes, positions, toponyms) and poetic language ('white Ganges'):

> The shape of Asia is symmetrical to both
> continents, and from the other side is similar to a cone
> extending a little up to the edge of the entire east.
> There stand the Pillars of the Theban Dionysus
> by the waters of the extreme Ocean,
> near the most remote Indian Mountains, where the white Ganges
> rolls down its water to the Nysaean coast.
>
> (620–626)

Dionysius' important position in Rome and the dedication of his poem to Hadrian show how difficult it is to identify a clear-cut division between 'Greek' and 'Roman' geographies, at least in the imperial age (1.4).

[22] For the text, see *SH* F 23–38.
[23] For the text, see Courtney (1993), 247–253.
[24] For the text, see *GGM* 2.103–176; Jacob (1990); Brodersen (1994a); Bowie (2004); Hunter (2004); Amato (2005).

Two hundred years later, Postumius Rufius Festus Avienus of Volsinii (340–380 CE) translated Dionysius' poem into Latin, and produced a *Descriptio Orbis Terrae* of which 1,394 hexameters survive. Avienus also composed an iambic poem of his own – *Ora Maritima* ('Sea coasts') – in the form of a *periplous* surveying the coast from Massalia to Gades.[25] Avienus cites a long list of sources, from Hecataeus of Miletus, Herodotus and Thucydides to relatively obscure authors such as Bacoris of Rhodes and Cleon of Sicily (line 82 onward). This fact, along with the content of his poem, shows that Avienus assembled earlier bits of information and did not add new facts. His contribution thus lies mainly in his selection of material, as defined by his personal knowledge and scholarly orientation, and in his translation skills.

Poems of this sort did not offer a revolutionary attitude toward geography nor include striking new information. Indeed, they were quite traditional in arrangement, order and detail. Their uniqueness lay seemingly in the poetic format, but given the numerous Hellenistic and Roman examples of this phenomenon, this too was perhaps not so extraordinary. In all these cases, the authors must have had a choice between prose and poetry and could, with more ease and elaboration, have used the descriptive style of the historiographic tradition (2.2). Instead, they chose the genre of poetic geography, which seems less obvious to the modern mind. From our point of view, it is surprising to find poetry used in a field that requires factual accuracy without excessive information, let alone linguistic ornamentation. This would seem to apply even more in the case of mathematical geography. None the less, and as has been shown above, in the Hellenistic and Roman periods in particular some authors chose to convey geographical data in poetry. These were not simply sporadic passing references to geographical matters interwoven into poetry, but entire texts (usually hexametric or iambic) that focused on geography.

One might claim that geography was the main focus of such poems, and that their authors were therefore primarily 'geographers', the metrical format being merely a form of window-dressing intended to ornament the style or attract an audience. But there are parallel cases of technical and didactic subjects discussed in a poetic format: astronomy by Aratus and Manilius; philosophy by Epicurus and Lucretius; and agriculture by Hesiod, Virgil and Columella.[26] Like these other authors, it seems, Pausanias of Damascus, the two Dionysii, Alexander 'Lychnos', Varro and Avienus chose poetry because of the literary challenge it posed them

[25] For the text, see *GGM* 2.177–189; Holder (1965).
[26] Harder *et al.* (2009); Taub (2009).

and to the educated portion of their readership, and perhaps because the poetic form added entertainment value, making geography more digestible for other (perhaps smaller) portions of their audience. These authors are thus best understood as poets who challenged themselves to versify particularly complex themes, and who turned this ability into a virtue demonstrating their literary skill. Once again, it seems that there was no match between geographical content and any specific genre, and despite the existence of numerous geographical texts in prose – perhaps the majority of those produced – it was clearly acceptable to compose poetry with geographical content.

These authors' choices and interests were fundamentally different from those of poets who used geographical information only sporadically. Even so, whatever the poets' intentions, ample geographical data were included in other poetic corpora.[27] The ancients had already noticed the potential for extracting geographical data from poetry. Alexander Polyhistor, for instance, composed a treatise *On Places Mentioned by Alcman* (*FGrHist* 273 F 95–96), while Strabo often quoted poetic verses for their geographical significance.[28] A few examples will illustrate this tendency.

As the title of Alexander's lost work on Alcman hints, the geographical value of poetry can be estimated simply through its references to sites and nations, which reveal patterns of toponymy and boundaries of geographical knowledge at a specific point in time, particularly when rare names are mentioned. Poets may also exploit the inherent descriptive essence of verse and its rich verbal texture to describe landscapes or to illustrate distances using the technique of *ekphrasis*, 'extended description'. Although accuracy is not necessarily the main goal of many poets, some examples display the geographical potential in poetry. The first is Alcaeus, *c.* 600 BCE, on the Hebrus River (modern Maritsa, in Bulgaria):

> Hebrus, you flow, the most beautiful of rivers,
> past Aenus into the turbid sea,
> surging through the land of Thrace.
> (Alkaios F 45 Campbell)

The second is Pindar, on Mount Aetna, in Sicily:

> Snow-clad Aetna, who nurses her keen frost for the live-long year,
> from whose inmost caves burst forth the purest founts of
>   unapproachable fire,
> and, in the day-time, her rivers roll a lurid stream of smoke,

---

[27] Samples from Greek poetry appear in Warmington (1934), 77–81.
[28] Dueck (2005a).

> while amid the gloom of night, the ruddy flame,
> as it sweeps along, with crashing din carries rocks to the
> deep sea far below.
>
> (Pind. *Pyth.* 1.20–24)

So too Greek drama, both tragedy and comedy, occasionally included geographical facts, often intermingled with fantasy. This has two consequences: the dating of a play can sometimes be established by analysis of how the incorporated fragments of geographical description reflect the state of geographical knowledge at a particular point in time, and the geographical data included in dated plays can help reconstruct geographical notions and the extent of spatial expansion at the time they were written.[29]

It was particularly in Hellenistic Alexandria that a literary trend evolved for including geographical references in poetry to convey specific ideas or to ornament the work with archaic toponyms. Such conventions included descriptions of scenery and landscape for decorative purposes (*ekphraseis*).[30] Roman poets imitated these Alexandrian trends, and their poems reveal artistic delight both in using earlier Greek poetic names – Thynus for Bithynia (Catullus 25.7), or the Cytaeis for the people of Colchis (Propertius 2.4.7) – and in expressing Roman pride via allusions to newly acquired regions, by showing off toponyms and ethnonyms of recently subdued nations such as the Britanni (Lucretius 6.1106) or the Seres of China (Virg. *Georg.* 2.121).[31]

More than the specific poetic genre (epic, lyric or drama), the political and social environment in which poems were composed influenced the nature of their geographical allusions. Thus Roman poetry, even when it responded to Greek models on a stylistic level, reflected realities and ideas from its own time. Catullus (no. 11) asked his friends to deliver a message to his mistress and, to demonstrate their special loyalty, he described how they would accompany him to the remotest parts of the world, using geographical markers that described regions recently conquered by Rome:

> Furius and Aurelius, who will be Catullus's fellow travellers,
> whether he makes his way even to distant India,
> where the shore is beaten by the far-resounding eastern wave,
> or to Hyrcania and soft Arabia,
> or to the Sacae and the archer Parthians,
> or to those plains that the seven-fold Nile dyes with his flood,
> or whether he will tramp across the high Alps

[29] Hall (1987); Finkelberg (1998); Bonnafé (2000); Futo Kennedy (2006).
[30] Krevans (1983), esp. 204–212 on Theocritus.
[31] Mayer (1986).

to visit the memorials of great Caesar,
the Gaulish Rhine, the formidable Britons, most remote of men.

This is a clear case of geographical reality reflected in a non-geographical context. Roman poets tended to insert names of distant lands and strange peoples to celebrate national conquests, but also to ornament their works. In addition, the practice allowed them to demonstrate their erudition, by imitating earlier Greek conventions of inserting geographical names, and by alluding to recent territorial additions to the Empire.[32] These tendencies are particularly apparent at times when foreign wars were under way, or on the occasion of individual victories. In such circumstances, poets would sometimes reflect the excitement of space and distance by alluding to remote toponyms and ethnonyms, or by exploiting poetic licence by adding elements of fantasy. Virgil, Horace, Propertius, Ovid and Seneca reacted to specific political developments that had geographical significance, such as Lucullus' campaign beyond the Euphrates (Plut. *Luc.* 24.4–8), Pompey's actions in the Caucasus and along the Caspian (Dio Cass. 37.1.5), and the victories of Augustus.[33] In his *Aeneid*, Virgil consciously and deliberately adopted and imitated entire sections of Homeric poetry. These included the lists in catalogue form of Roman ancestors and their rivals, the native Latins, and the triumphal procession on the shield of Aeneas forged by Vulcan. But Virgil gave the latter description contemporary geographical overtones:

> The conquered peoples move in long array,
> as diverse in fashion of dress and arms as in tongue.
> Here Mulciber had portrayed the Nomad race and the ungirt Africans,
> here the Leleges and Carians and quivered Gelonians.
> Euphrates moved now with humbler waves,
> and the Morini were there, furthest of mankind, and the
>   Rhine of double horn,
> the untamed Dahae, and Araxes chafing at his bridge.
>
> (*Aen.* 8.722–728)

Similarly, when Virgil depicts Aeneas meeting his father Anchises in the underworld, the old man reveals the geographical extent of the future empire in the time of Augustus, including sites and peoples in numerous remote parts of the world (*Aen.* 6.792–805).[34] The same Augustan

---

[32] Meyer (1961); Thomas (1982); Syme (1987); Grant (2000).

[33] Hardie (1986); Syme (1987); Nicolet (1991); Dueck (2003).

[34] Virgil's depiction of an underworld organized in different sections also reflects his spatial sense of geography. See Feldherr (1999).

atmosphere of unprecedented political and geographical achievement is apparent in the poems of Horace:

> At you marvels the Cantabrian never before subdued,
> at you the Mede and Indian, at you the roaring Scythian,
> you mighty guardian
> of Italy and of imperial Rome.
> To you the Nile gives ear, the Nile that hides the sources of its springs,
> to you the Danube, the swirling Tigris,
> the Ocean teeming with monsters
> that roars around the distant Britons.
> To you the land of Gaul that recks not death
> and stubborn Iberia,
> before you stand in awe the slaughter-loving Sygambri
> with weapons laid to rest.
>
> (Hor. *Carm.* 4.14.41–52)

So too Ovid:

> Is it indeed a greater thing to have subdued the sea-girt Britons,
> to have led his victorious fleet up the seven-mouthed stream
>   of the papyrus-bearing Nile, to have added the rebellious Numidians,
> Iouba of Cinyps, and Pontus, swelling with threats
> of the mighty name of Mithridates, to the sway of the people of Quirinus,
> to have celebrated some triumphs and to have earned many more,
> than to have begotten so great a man? With him, as ruler
>   of the world,
> you have indeed, o heavenly ones, showered rich blessings
>   upon the human race.
>
> (Ov. *Met.* 15.752–759)

It is thus apparent that geographical information, particularly in the form of names of sites and nations, was widely exploited by poets for the sake of exotic ornamentation, and, in the case of Roman poets in the first century BCE, probably for ideological meaning as revealed through geographical markers.

It is hard to know how many of these names readers could actually identify and mentally locate. Authors may well have expected their audience to recognize such names at some level (e.g., by their sound, meaning, location). But it is equally possible that accurate knowledge was not needed to achieve the desired effect of awe and excitement, and that the sound of a foreign name in itself was intended to create a powerful image.

A combination of fact and fantasy characterized early popular myths. Fear of the unknown and emphasis on the courage of legendary heroes fuelled the exploitation of geographical landmarks to highlight dramatic elements. In some periods of antiquity, 'newer myths' were created around military achievements associated with wide geographical horizons, for example, the legends woven around the character of Alexander the Great and the mythical atmosphere that surrounded Roman conquests. In the period when the earliest myths were formed, however, two other types of geographical expression emerged: strictly factual reports of coastal voyages (*periploi*) and Presocratic investigation, which became the basis for geography with pretension to being scientific (chapter 3).

2.2 THE HISTORIOGRAPHIC TRADITION

Any event in the universe occurs at a specific point in time and space, and both dimensions, the chronological and the physical, are essential to understanding and defining such events, be they personal or national. Only if one knows *when* and *where* something took place can one fully absorb it. This explains the formation of a major branch of geography within historiographic frameworks.[35] It is generally recognized that written histories in antiquity were based on simple pre-existing chronological and genealogical lists. The latter, compiled by logographers or chroniclers, gradually turned into 'history' by becoming more voluminous and elaborate in terms of literary style and in the search for causation and explanation. A parallel development can be traced for geography: basic building blocks of practical, catalogue-style information created the foundation for texts that were richer both verbally and intellectually. The evolution of this branch of descriptive geography thus depends on earlier prototypes and is closely affiliated to historiography (see also 1.2).

The cornerstone for the close conceptual and literary link between history and geography is preserved in the first coherent historiographic work, that of Herodotus of Halicarnassus (*c.* 484–428 BCE). Herodotus himself, however, refers back several times to his predecessor, Hecataeus of Miletus who, half a century earlier, created a compilation that may reasonably be regarded as the seed of descriptive geography. Hecataeus (*c.* 550–490 BCE) travelled in Greece, Asia Minor, the Black Sea and Egypt, and produced a work traditionally titled *periodos gês* ('circuit of the earth') or *periêgêsis* ('outline').[36] This was a list of coastal sites that included details of

---

[35] Clarke (1999), 1–77; Merrills (2005); Dench (2007); Engels (2007); Purves (2010).
[36] For the text, see *FGrHist* 1 F 37–357: F 37–194 (Europe); F 195–299 (Asia); F 300–324 (Egypt); F 325–328 (Ethiopia); F 329–357 (Libya). See also Caspari (1910). Hecataeus also produced a corrected and enlarged version of Anaximander's map.

directions of travel, local mythology and ethnography, and topographical remarks such as the situation of rivers, mountains and gulfs. The work maintained a coastal geographical order and was arranged in two books, one devoted to Europe, the other to Asia. Hecataeus did not recognize Africa (Libya) as a separate continent, and included his impressions of Egypt in his survey of Asia. Most surviving fragments of the work are preserved as short entries in Stephanus of Byzantium's sixth-century CE geographical lexicon *Ethnika*. Thus for example:

> SICANE: a *polis* in Iberia; thus Hecataeus [says] in 'Europe' (F 45).
> CYLLANDUS: a *polis* in Caria; thus Hecataeus [says] in 'Asia' (F 250).
> CATHELIA: a *polis* near Carthage; Hecataeus [says] in 'Asia' (F 338a).

Hecataeus' *periêgêsis* thus incorporated order, grouping, and minimal description of individual places. Herodotus took these contributions further, by following Hecataeus' footsteps both literally – he too travelled to Egypt – and intellectually.[37] In an effort to explain the clash between the Greek world and the Persian Empire in the first few decades of the fifth century BCE, he tried for the first time to approach geographical and ethnographic themes systematically. Unlike earlier *periploi*, which were practical in both their goals and their origins (2.3), Herodotus aspired primarily to document the war that united certain Greeks in defence of their homeland against the imperial aspirations of the Persian king. Herodotus' broad-minded approach meant that he went back centuries in time to explain 'for what reason they fought one other' (1.1), and that he attempted to set events against the broadest possible geographical and ethnographic background. The Persian Empire in this period encompassed many regions and peoples and required a great breadth of description. Not only did Herodotus offer an unprecedented amount of detail, therefore, but the very need to arrange and order such information was a novelty.

Herodotus wanted to give his audience a comprehensive idea of the spatial extent of the Persian Empire and of the variety of its inhabitants. He accordingly devoted four of his nine books to presenting this framework, and systematically described the various Persian satrapies (administrative districts), including the nature of the lands and their inhabitants. The material is generally arranged in the same order: first, the physical features of the land, including its topography, climate and distinctive fauna

---

[37] Gould (1989), esp. 86–109; Romm (1989a); (1998); (2006); Rood (2006). For his travels, see Lisler (1980); Brown (1988); Montiglio (2000); (2006); and the sceptic view in Armayor (1978); (1980a); (1980b); (1985).

and flora; and then a detailed description of the inhabitants, including their origin and their habits in regard to nutrition, marriage and sexual intercourse, social groupings, clothing, death and burial.

The mix of concepts in Herodotus' work allows his approach to be treated as a product of two coinciding tendencies: archaic-mythic-epic geography and the beginnings of scientific-empirical geography. It is in Herodotus' work that the term *oikoumenê* ('inhabited' sc. world) is first attested, and the author treats inhabited land as a synonym for the world (e.g. 3.106). Throughout the development of ancient geography, the physical boundaries of the earth were connected inseparably with demographic borders of habitation.[38] Herodotus modified the Homeric concept of a world composed of land surrounded by Ocean, and claimed instead that deserts rimmed the *oikoumenê* and that only beyond these came the waters of the surrounding Ocean (as implied at e.g. 4.18).

Herodotus' approach served as inspiration for later historians who could not, or would not, ignore geographical factors. Such authors, however, did develop the technique, adding tones and emphases that fitted their own goals and scholarly personalities. There is no point in mentioning all the Greek and Roman historians whose work touches on geographical matters. But several deserve special attention because of their personal touch and the novelties they added to the genre. Thucydides, for example, never devoted specific sections of his history to geographical details, but he moulded them into the text as an inseparable matter-of-fact part of the body of evidence.[39] Like Herodotus, Thucydides focused on a war (the so-called Peloponnesian War, between Athens, Sparta and their allies), but he was one of the first authors to link geographical elements with various human phenomena:[40] the economic prosperity of Corinth as a result of its location on an isthmus (1.13.5); the dangers of sailing through the Strait of Messina (4.24.5); and the tactical considerations behind the Pylos affair (4.3.2–3). Thucydides was apparently uninterested in detailed spatial and geographical description, and used such data merely for short explanatory excerpts. The following paragraph is exceptional, and proves that he knew how to offer such material even if he generally chose not to do so:

[38] The edges of the world were often associated with the same nations and defined according to their situation. See 3.1.

[39] Pearson (1939); Sieveking (1964); Funke and Haake (2006); Pothou (2009), 49–71.

[40] See the discussion of deterministic climatic theory in chapter 3.

The river Acheloüs ... passes by the city of Stratus high up the stream, but by Oeniadae empties into the sea, where it surrounds the city with marshes ... most of the Echinades islands lie opposite to Oeniadae at no great distance from the mouth of the Acheloüs, so that the river, which is large, keeps making fresh deposits of silt, and some of the islands have already become part of the mainland ... the stream is wide, deep and turbid, and the islands are close together and serve to bind to one another the bars as they are formed, preventing them from being broken up, since the islands lie not in a line but irregularly, and do not allow straight channels for the water into the open sea. These islands are uninhabited and not large. (2.102.2–4)

Like Herodotus, Thucydides presented Greece as a familiar environment inhabited by ordinary people, as opposed to other parts of the world. The latter were less well-known and less central to the historian's focus, requiring a different type of description.

Xenophon's *Anabasis* offers a detailed account of travels in a historiographic framework.[41] Xenophon, who personally experienced the events, described the march of a group of Greek mercenaries who became stranded in the heart of the Persian Empire in 401 BCE. His goal was to convey to his readers the details of the topography and itinerary of this extraordinary journey back to the Greek world:[42]

From there [the Greeks] marched through the land of the Chalybians seven stages, fifty parasangs ... [the Chalybians] had corselets of linen reaching down to the groin with a thick fringe of plaited cords instead of flaps ... leaving this land the Greeks arrived at the Harpasus river, which was four plethra in width. From there they marched through the territory of the Scuthenoi four stages, twenty parasangs over a level plain ... from there they journeyed four stages, twenty parasangs, to a large and prosperous inhabited city called Gumnias. (*Anab.* 4.7.15–19)

Another Greek who visited and in fact remained in the east was Ctesias of Cnidus (early fourth century BCE). Ctesias was the personal physician of the Persian king Artaxerxes II. This position allowed him to observe parts of the Persian empire at first-hand, and supplied the background for his literary works.[43] Ctesias composed a *Persika*, in which he described Persian history, including some geographical and ethnographic details, among them a (now lost) list of places and distances in the Persian Empire. Other geographically significant works were his *Indika* and a *periplous*. Because

---

[41] Manfredi (1986); Baslez (1995).
[42] There is no reason to believe that Alexander of Macedon read Xenophon's *Anabasis* as a guidebook: McGroarty (2006).
[43] *FGrHist* 688; Lenfant (2004); (2011).

Persia and India were exotic places from a Greek perspective, many details in Ctesias' surveys were regarded as marvels or even incredible. This sense was enhanced by his exaggeration of details, as well as by his simple misunderstandings and consequent erroneous descriptions of unusual sights.

A few decades later, in the mid-fourth century BCE, Ephorus of Cyme made two original contributions to descriptive geography.[44] He arranged his 30-book historiographic work by geographical area (Greece, Sicily, Persia and Macedon)[45] and devoted Books 4 and 5 to a geographical survey of the *oikoumenē*. The novelty was that instead of inserting geographical excerpts within his historiographic survey, as Herodotus had, Ephorus concentrated the relevant geographical material in individual books, one dealing with Europe (Book 4), the other with Asia (Book 5). Only fragments of Ephorus' work survive, but these literary devices seem to have allowed him to offer more detail and to deal with broader issues without distracting the reader from his primary interest, his historiographic survey. Both Herodotus and Ephorus recognized the importance of geographical knowledge, although they chose to approach it in different ways.

A development that literally changed the world, while incidentally affecting ancient geography, was the military and political accomplishments of Alexander the Great of Macedon.[46] Alexander's vast conquests expanded intellectual horizons, and some ancient sources suggest that this was achieved not as a by-product of this territorial expansion, but as the outcome of a deliberate plan devised by the well-educated monarch. Alexander prepared grand strategies and well-trained armies, but he also took with him a large entourage that included scholars who were ordered to document every curiosity and natural phenomenon encountered in the course of the king's expeditions. Doubts have none the less been cast on this image of scientific patronage, suggesting either that the record-keeping was not planned systematically in advance, or that Alexander's prestige was appropriated by intellectuals in an attempt to magnify the significance of their own efforts.[47] Still, the active tendency of the king to also widen his mental horizons by promoting written records of actual experiences cannot be entirely misconceived.

In addition to records of the sailing trip through the Indus River to Persia (2.3), the main contribution of Alexander's historians to descriptive geography was their documentation of exotic local details, particularly in

[44] *FGrHist* 70; Barber (1979).
[45] Drews (1963).   [46] Geus (2003).   [47] Romm (1989b).

eastern regions such as India, and their recruitment of geographical information to glorify the king even if this involved a renunciation of straightforward truth:[48]

> They transferred the Caucasus to the region of the Indian mountains … which is more than thirty thousand *stadia* distant from India … for these were the farthermost mountains towards the east that were known to the writers of that time. (Strabo 11.5.5)

The Hellenistic age inherited from Alexander a much wider world, particularly in the east. Alexander's conquests also aroused intellectual interest and probably popular curiosity about landscapes and inhabitants of foreign countries.[49] The focus of new treatises accordingly turned to individual countries, which were surveyed not as part of a universal history but in separate monographs. Stylistically, these works adhered to the descriptive tradition of geography. Intellectual interest thus concentrated on narrower, regional histories, which unsurprisingly included details of local geography and introduced what was referred to as *chôrographia*, geographical description of a specific region (*chôra*) within the *oikoumenê*.

This development was enhanced by independent initiatives of Hellenistic monarchs to promote their political and economic power by expanding physical and intellectual horizons.[50] In Egypt, Ptolemy I *c.* 300 BCE offered Hecataeus of Abdera support to compose his *Aegyptiaka*, which described the geography of the country and the habits of its residents. Hecataeus also produced an entire work dealing with the semimythic northern nation of the Hyperboreans.[51] Works on India were produced in similar circumstances in two consecutive generations: in about 304 BCE, Megasthenes was sent as Seleucus I Nicator's ambassador to the court of Sandrocottus, king of Palimbothra in eastern India; and Deimachus served as the ambassador of Seleucus' heir, Antiochus Soter, to the court of Sandrocottus' son, King Allitrochadas of Palimbothra. Both Megasthenes and Deimachus recorded their impressions and reported on research they conducted on Indian affairs.[52] Megasthenes produced four books, in which he thoroughly described India's geography and fauna and flora, and the social structures and customs of the country's inhabitants and their history.[53] This was the first direct written testimony by

[48] Brown (1949); Pearson (1983); Aerts (1994).
[49] Fraser (1972).
[50] For royal sponsorship of exploratory expeditions, see 3.3.
[51] *FGrHist* 264 F 7–14; Dillery (1998).
[52] Ptolemy II also sent a certain Dionysius to India (Plin. *HN* 6.58).
[53] *FGrHist* 715; Brown (1955); (1957); Majumdar (1958); Bosworth (1996).

an individual from the west who visited the Ganges valley. Megasthenes mixed his own experiences, interviews with local Indian scholars and details taken from earlier Greek records. This mixture was sometimes regarded with contempt by later authors:

But especially do Deimachus and Megasthenes deserve to be distrusted. For they are the persons who tell us about the Enotokoites ('men who sleep in their ears') and the Astomoi ('mouthless men') and Arrhinae ('noseless men'), and about Monophthalmoi ('men with one eye'), Makroskeleis ('men with long legs') and Opisthodaktyloi ('men with fingers turned backwards'). (Strabo 2.1.9)

Megasthenes' now-fragmentary work none the less preserves invaluable information. (The work of Deimachus is lost.)

As Hellenism spread in the east, Rome gradually expanded beyond the Italian peninsula, as a result of the Punic Wars. Confronted by this increasing power, Polybius attempted to explain how Rome grew so rapidly. To this end, he composed his *Histories*, although he also dealt with geography, which he regarded as an essential component of historiography:[54]

Systematic history consists of three parts, the first being the industrious study of memoirs and other documents and a comparison of their contents; the second the survey of cities, places, rivers, lakes and in general all the peculiar features of land and sea and the distance of one place from another; and the third being the review of political events. (12.25e.1)

This perception pertained particularly to the description of battles:

We must by no means neglect to illustrate by local descriptions events of any sort, and least of all those of a war, nor must we hesitate to adopt as landmarks harbours, seas, and islands, or again temples, mountains, and local names of districts, and finally differences of climate, as these latter are most universally recognized by mankind. (5.21.6)

Polybius had both practical and intellectual qualifications which enabled him to undertake an extensive geographical survey. First, he had travelled widely, joining Scipio Aemilianus, his Roman captor who became his friend, in his journeys to Spain, Gaul, the Alps and Africa. In addition, Scipio sponsored a fleet that allowed Polybius to make a voyage of discovery to Africa (Plin. *HN* 5.9). Polybius was also qualified in astronomy and geometry, and composed (now lost) geographical works such as *On the Inhabiting of the Equatorial Region* (34.1.7) and a *periplous*. It was with

---

[54] Walbank (1948); Pédech (1956); Clarke (1999), 77–128.

these tendencies that Polybius approached geographical themes in his historiographic work. Most likely following Ephorus in this regard, he too decided to reduce (although not to omit entirely) geographical digressions within the general flow of his survey, and to devote a separate section to geographical matters, to help his readers understand broader background issues:

> I have omitted these subjects not because I think they are foreign to my history, but in the first place because I did not wish to be constantly interrupting the narrative and distracting readers from the actual subject, and next because I decided not to make scattered and casual allusions to such matters, but assigning the proper place and time to their special treatment to give as true an account of all as is in my power. (3.57.4–5)

Polybius accordingly assembled all this information in Book 34 of his *Histories*. The book is lost, but there is considerable evidence about its content and Polybius' approach to traditional geographical themes. As the historian most associated with the idea of pragmatic history, Polybius concentrated less on geographical theories and scientific calculations, and focused instead on information useful to his intended readership, mainly facts about remote places. Book 34 therefore contained a systematic overview of the *oikoumenê* and a detailed description (*chôrographia*) of Europe and Africa as the two continents relevant to the Punic Wars. Emphasizing practical details of distances and topography, Polybius criticized predecessors who dealt only with theoretical geography. He assigned importance to Homer in the tradition of Greek geography, and used both the *Iliad* and the *Odyssey* for geographical information. A significant part of his discussion was devoted to the assumed location of sites Odysseus encountered in his wanderings. Another issue was the climate–character connection, in which Polybius proposed a division of the globe into six rather than five zones (3.2).

A central author in the tradition of descriptive geography was Posidonius of Apamea.[55] Posidonius was first and foremost a philosopher, and as such he had an especially broad intellectual scope and an interest in explaining natural phenomena. He therefore surveyed some problems in physical or scientific geography, for example tides and volcanic events. The evidence suggests that it was rare to find such a combination of scientific and descriptive tendencies in one individual. Scholars usually tended either in the mathematical direction, immersing themselves entirely in quantitative themes (chapter 3), or were devoted to the descriptive branch,

---

[55] *FGrHist* 87; Edelstein and Kidd (1972); Pédech (1974); Clarke (1999), 129–192.

often after or simultaneously, with a historiographical career.[56] Posidonius revealed his multiple interests in his *On Ocean* and in his calculation of the earth's circumference. He also made several new contributions to geography. The first was to approach the analysis of geographical space through structures, beginning with larger units and moving to smaller ones: latitudinal zones, then continents, then countries, regions and cities. This geographically reversed pyramid of structures replaced the traditional linear concept of the *periploi*. Second, Posidonius treated time as an important factor in the transformation of physical and human geography. This idea also appears in Strabo, who was perhaps influenced in this respect by Posidonius:

The man who busies himself with the description (*periodos*) of the earth must speak not only of the facts of the present, but sometimes also of facts of the past, especially when they are notable. (Strabo 6.1.2)

Posidonius thus emphasized the cyclical dynamics of tides and the temporal element in demographic changes caused by emigration and war. Third, he attempted to pinpoint general, repeated systems of operation for natural phenomena so as to create theoretical models. Posidonius was motivated by a curious, inquisitive spirit, and based some of his observations on his extensive travels in Spain, Gaul, Italy and the East.

Over the course of more than four centuries, descriptive geography (as opposed to mathematical and cartographic geography), particularly in its 'historiographic' form, varied in three parameters: (1) focus: descriptions of regions within an *oikoumenic* scope, or chorographies within monographs devoted to individual countries; (2) literary position: sections with various levels of detail integrated into the historiographic train of events, or separate compositional units devoted to geographical matters; (3) perception of space: linear outlines versus spatial presentations. These forms produced the next generation of descriptive geographies, each of which had a unique agenda (although geography embedded in historiography persisted until late antiquity).

Born in Pontus in Asia Minor in around 64 BCE, Strabo of Amasia[57] travelled as an adult at least to Alexandria, some parts of Greece, and Rome. Strabo first composed a historiographic work (or more than one) in which he attempted to survey a number of chapters in world history, including the deeds of Alexander. Only later, possibly in the second

---

[56] Neither Polybius nor Strabo abandoned scientific issues entirely. But their tendency, by and large, was toward the literary-descriptive rather than the scientific-mathematical style.

[57] Clarke (1999), 193–336; Dueck (2000).

decade of the first century CE, did he compose his geographical *magnum opus*. Thus he too had a historiographic background but expressed his geographical interest in a separate and much more extended description.

Strabo's *Geography* comprised 17 books and surveyed the entire world known in his time, beginning at the Iberian peninsula, moving around the Mediterranean (Europe, Asia and Africa), and concluding in northwest Africa. The work was divided by region: Books 1 and 2, introductory remarks on geography, geographers, major trends in scientific and descriptive geography and criticism of predecessors; Book 3, Iberia and nearby islands; Book 4, Gaul, Britain, Ireland, Thule and the Alps; Books 5 and 6, Italy, Sicily, the islands between Sicily and North Africa; Book 7, German tribes, Pannonia, Illyria, Macedonia and Thrace; Books 8–10, Greece; Books 11–14, Asia Minor; Book 15, India and Persia; Book 16, Mesopotamia, Syria, Phoenicia, Judaea, the Persian Gulf and Arabia; Book 17, Egypt, Ethiopia and Libya.

Strabo followed the descriptive tradition, which meant that he included local detail regarding flora and fauna, shapes of both borderlines and topographies, mythology, history and ethnography. The value of his *Geography* resides in its broad scope, while its novelty lies in undertaking a description of the entire world (i.e. not local geography/chorography) and one not subjected to historiography. The work also preserves many remnants of lost geographies, and sums up centuries of geographical traditions. Although Strabo declared himself uninterested in practising scientific geography, he none the less devoted a significant portion of his first two books to summarizing the scientific achievements and ideas that had been reached before him. Nor could he entirely ignore some issues on the fringes of science throughout his entire survey.[58] In a sense, therefore, his *Geography* became an encyclopaedic contribution containing details of all sorts.

Another important feature of Strabo's *Geography* is that his geographical survey reflects the political reality of his time. Living in the first century BCE, at a time when Rome under Augustus was establishing itself as a world power, Strabo absorbed the new situation. He included hints of his generation's admiration for Augustus, who 'ruled like a father' (6.4.2), and expressed the connection between politics and geography by identifying the borders of the *oikoumenê* with the limits of the Roman Empire:

The spread of the empires of the Romans and the Parthians has presented to geographers of today a considerable addition to our empirical knowledge of

[58] Strabo 1.1.14; 2.5.2; 2.5.34; Aujac (1966); Dueck (2000).

geography, just as did the campaign of Alexander to geographers of earlier times. (1.2.1)

More or less simultaneously, Iouba II king of Mauretania and Libya (*c.* 50 BCE–23 CE) contributed his own genius to the political and scholarly world of the first century CE.[59] Iouba was displayed as a captive in the African triumph of Julius Caesar in 46 BCE. He then grew up in the house of Octavia, won Roman citizenship and became a friend and client of Augustus. He was educated along Hellenistic lines, and became a prolific author interested in themes including theatre, painting, history and geography. Iouba was eventually appointed king of Mauretania, and promoted scholarship there by establishing a library and initiating journeys of discovery (2.3). His geographical research included information he sent to M. Agrippa for his own geographical project; a commentary on the voyage of Hanno the Carthaginian; and three ethnographic regional works (*Libyka*, *Assyriaka* and *Arabika*). Most of what we have of his work is preserved by Pliny the Elder, for example:

About the Fortunate Islands, Iouba has ascertained the following facts: they lie in a south-westerly direction, at a distance of 625 miles' sail from the Purple Islands, provided that a course is laid north of due west for 250 miles and then east for 375 miles; that the first island reached is called Ombrios, and there are no traces of buildings upon it, but it has a pool surrounded by mountains, and trees resembling giant fennel … and that visible from these islands is Ninguaria, so named from its perpetual snow, and wrapped in cloud; and next to it one named Canaria, from its multitude of dogs of a huge size, two of which were brought back for Iouba. He said that in this island there are traces of buildings; that while they all have an abundant supply of fruit and birds of every kind, Canaria also abounds in palm-groves bearing dates … and that these islands are plagued with the rotting carcasses of monstrous creatures that are constantly being cast ashore by the sea. (*HN* 6.203–205)

The descriptive branch of geography thus departed from the historiographic tradition. Geographical digressions within historiographic works persisted into later antiquity (Dio Cassius in Greek and Ammianus Marcellinus in Latin), but some descriptive geographies were produced free of historiographic context. The roots of descriptive geography were in the historiographic tradition, in the choice of vocabulary, the attempt to offer elaborate reports of things that were seen, and attention to the description itself. But when the style became independent, authors added

---

[59] For the text, see *FGrHist* 275; Roller (2003); (2004).

their own individual emphases. This was still literary prose, but the focus changed as the geographical theme came to the fore.

As with other literary genres, Roman authors of historiographic surveys adopted Greek conventions to include geographical sections. Sallust, for example, in his *Jugurthan War* devoted three chapters (17–19) to the land and people of north Africa, which was the scene of the narrative.[60] Because Sallust dealt with a specific topic and did not share Polybius' broad, universal approach, geography had a narrower role in his monograph, and he introduces the section as a mere digression required by convention:

> My subject seems to call for a brief account of the geography of Africa and some description of the nations there with whom the people of Rome has had wars or alliances. Of those regions and peoples, however, which are seldom visited because of the heat, the difficulty of access, or the stretches of desert, I could not easily give an account based upon certain information. The rest I shall dispatch in the fewest possible words. (*Iug.* 17.1–2)

This digression may have an additional purpose: emphasizing the relationship between the physical features of the place and the character of its rough, hardy, untamed people. Like Herodotus in his presentation of the clash between Asia and Europe during the Persian Wars, Sallust hinted at a conflict between Italy and Africa representing a clash between civilization and barbarism.

Julius Caesar offers a unique variety of descriptive geography reflecting his perspective as a military leader.[61] Unlike historians who gathered information from written sources, Caesar reported his own experiences in the field, for which he adopted a brief, pointed style. In the *Gallic War* he refers constantly to topographic and ethnographic circumstances, including distances in territories he occupied or bypassed, suggesting that successful military action enhanced geographical knowledge. The famous opening sentence of Caesar's commentaries is purely geographical: 'All Gallia is divided into three parts' (1.1). The section that follows describes the territory further:

> The Helvetii are closely confined by the nature of their territory. On one side is the river Rhine, exceedingly broad and deep, which separates the Helvetian territory from the Germans; on another, the Jura range, exceedingly high, lying between the Sequani and the Helvetii; on the third, the lake of Geneva and the river Rhône, which separates the Roman province from the Helvetii. (*BGall.* 1.2)

These comments ('broad', 'deep', 'high') suggest the perspective of an actual witness to the topography. They reveal an awareness of borders

---

[60] Scanlon (1988); Green (1993).   [61] Krebs (2006).

determined by natural topography: by rivers, a lake or mountain ranges. And the passage concludes with an explanation of the inhabitants' political and social behaviour: the Helvetians were confined in their territory by nature itself, a circumstance that put them under stress and spurred them to set out on the military expeditions that led to Roman intervention. This excerpt thus contains a number of important notions of geopolitics, in the sense that geography is taken to influence political developments.

Toward the end of his life, at the age of 76, Augustus publicly presented a summary of his achievements. In the so-called *Res Gestae*, the *princeps* consistently exploits toponyms as landmarks for his expansive influence on world affairs (sections 26–33).[62] The document thus uses geographical terminology to deliver its message, for example:

I extended the boundaries of all the provinces … The provinces of the Gauls, the Hispanias and Germany, bounded by the Ocean from Gades to the mouth of the Elbe, I reduced to a state of peace. The Alps, from the region that lies nearest to the Adriatic as far as the Tuscan Sea, I brought to a state of peace … My fleet sailed from the mouth of the Rhine eastward as far as the lands of the Cimbri into which, up to that time, no Roman had ever penetrated by land or sea; and the Cimbri, Charydes, Semnones and other peoples of the Germans of the same region, through their envoys, sought my friendship and that of the Roman people. On my order and under my auspices two armies were led, at almost the same time, into Ethiopia and Arabia … Ethiopia was penetrated as far as the town of Nabata, which is next to Meroe. In Arabia, the army advanced into the territories of the Sabaei to the town of Mariba. (section 26)

Unlike the documentary, historiographic orientation of Caesar and Augustus, Pomponius Mela exploited the descriptive style for his geographical survey of the world (*c.* 37–41 CE).[63] The designation of the work as *De chorographia* is in fact self-contradictory, since a *chorographia* by definition aims at a detailed description of one particular region within the world. This may only show, however, that there was no generally agreed-upon terminology for such works. Mela's purpose was similar to Strabo's: to describe the entire world. But the size of the works and the level of detail were very different: Mela's *De chorographia* was far more condensed and limited than Strabo's *Geography*. Book 1 surveyed the regions from the Pillars of Heracles through North Africa and Egypt to Asia Minor. Book 2 began in Scythia and Thrace, and proceeded through Europe back to the Pillars. It then offered a separate section on islands (2.97 and

[62] Nicolet (1991), 15–28.
[63] Brodersen (1994b); Romer (1998); Batty (2000).

following). Book 3 described the outer coasts of the *oikoumenê*, beginning with the Pillars and continuing along the coasts of the Iberian Peninsula. Mela combined myth with geography, indicating for example that the northern edge of the world was uninhabitable because of the presence of gold-guarding griffins (Mela 2.1). He also preserved different layers of data via the presentation of distances in terms of days of hiking (Mela 2.6), in *stades* (Mela 1.67) and in Roman miles (Mela 2.4).

A few decades later, Cornelius Tacitus (*c.* 55–120 CE) composed two monographs with strong ethnographic and geographical emphases. In his *Agricola*, Tacitus surveyed the conquests of his father-in-law Cn. Iulius Agricola, who served as governor of Britain. The work includes sections on the physical character of Britain and its inhabitants (*Agr.* 10–12), and emphasizes the existence of new geographical horizons:

It was only under Agricola that the Roman fleet for the first time rounded this coast, the coast of the remotest sea, and established the insularity of Britain. By the same voyage it discovered the islands called the Orcades [modern Orkneys], up to that time unknown, and conquered them. (*Agr.* 10)

The result, based on earlier sources, both Greek (Pytheas) and Roman (Caesar), included traditional geographical themes: land, people, climate and *paradoxa* (2.3). The *Germania* had an openly ethnographic focus, describing the nature and habits of the German tribes with a mix of admiration for their simple, modest ways, and reservations about their unrefined habits:

Next to the Chatti come the Usipi and Tencteri, on the Rhine banks where the river has ceased to shift its bed and has become fit to serve as a frontier. The Tencteri, in addition to the general reputation of the race as warriors, excel in the accomplishments of trained horsemen. (*Germ.* 32)

Tacitus incorporates sporadic geographical information in his historio-graphic works. The most famous of these is the ethnographic digression on the Jews and Judaea in the *Histories* (*Hist.* 5.2–13), in which he deals with traditional ethnographic themes but does not connect local traits and ethnic character, as he does with other nations.[64]

An important descriptive composition with strong geographical signifi-cance was the *Natural History* of Pliny the Elder (*c.* 23–79 CE).[65] The work is a massive encyclopaedic compilation of information, in 37 books, about the physical world rather than specifically about geography. Several books

---

[64] Bloch (2000).
[65] Detlefsen (1972); Shaw (1981); Beagon (1992); Healy (1999); Murphy (2004).

within it, however, patently take up geographical themes: Book 2, for example, deals with cosmology, astronomy and geology, while Books 3–6 include a geographical survey of the known world (Book 3 on Hispania, Italy and Sicily; Book 4 on Germania, the British Isles, Greece, the Black Sea regions and the Scythians; Book 5 on Africa including Egypt, Syria, Judaea, Asia Minor and Cyprus; Book 6 on Ethiopia, Arabia, the Caspian Sea, Babylonia, India and China). Some sections of the books devoted to animals (8–11) and plants (12–19) also include local descriptions. Because Pliny exploited numerous sources, his work preserves many fragments of lost geographies, and his summary of them represents a useful compilation of themes.

Pliny's career shaped his interests and the intellectual work he produced. Born into a wealthy family in Novum Comum in northern Italy, he received a wide-ranging education in Rome and served as a procurator in Hispania, Africa and the Rhineland. He was also a member of Vespasian's council and dedicated his major work to Vespasian's son and successor Titus. Pliny's career enabled him to travel to Africa and Hispania, and perhaps elsewhere as well, and his impressions of these places must have influenced his interests, although he never discusses his personal experiences. Pliny relied on numerous sources, which are enumerated at the beginning of his encyclopaedia. There he also reveals his patriotism, as he opens with 'Europe, nurse of the race that has conquered all nations and by far the loveliest portion of the earth' (*HN* 3.5).

In his more 'geographical' sections, Pliny follows the descriptive style, and the *Natural History* can be defined as an extended descriptive list of inventories of natural phenomena. One example of his approach to topographic description is his picture of Mount Atlas in Africa:

It is from the midst of the sands, according to the story, that this mountain raises its head to the heavens; rugged and craggy on the side that looks toward the shores of the ocean to which it has given its name, while on that which faces the interior of Africa it is shaded by dense groves of trees, and refreshed by flowing streams; fruits of all kinds spring up there spontaneously, to such an extent as to more than satiate every possible desire. (*HN* 5.6)

Another excerpt, in which Pliny describes the Black Sea regions, gives a sense of his treatment of ethnographic material:

The remaining portion of these shores is peopled by savage nations, the Melanchlaeni and the Coraxi, who formerly dwelt in Dioscurias, near the river Anthemus, now deserted, but once a famous city; so much so, indeed, that we learn from Timosthenes that three hundred nations, all of different languages, were in the habit of resorting to it, and in later times we had there one hundred and thirty interpreters for the purpose of transacting business. (*HN* 6.15)

Let us conclude this section of our survey with a late antique author who adhered to the traditional Herodotean treatment of geographical issues within historiography after centuries of descriptive conventions. Ammianus Marcellinus (*c.* 330–391 CE), a Greek writing in Latin, described the 18 provinces of the Persian kingdom and their features, including rivers, distances, toponyms, distinctive sights and a survey of the habits of their populations (23.6.1–86). Intriguingly, he describes this section of his work as a 'brief digression' (*excessus celer*) (23.6.1), terminology which goes back to the emergence of geographical digressions as supplements to larger historiographic narratives.

From its Herodotean beginnings, geography adhered to its historiographic parent or, better put, its older sibling (1.2). Herodotus and his successors realized that topographic and ethnographic information was essential to understanding historical events and particularly battlefield strategy. The immense significance of such passages, and the elaborate and extended literary attention sometimes paid to them, suggest that the tendency of modern scholars to treat ethno-geographical sections in historiography as mere digressions or at best as ancillary chapters is misguided; the fact that these sections were not the focal goal of the works in which they were embedded does not reduce their importance. Such descriptive geographical sections gradually became independent; first as separate sections within a larger work (Ephorus, Polybius), and then as independent compositions devoted to geographical issues but keeping the historiographic descriptive style. This 'style' did not adopt the scientific practice of accurate calculations and elaborate theories based on logic. Nor did it assume the metrical form and metaphorical language of poetry, or the catalogue-style approach of *periploi* and itineraries. Like historiography, it used large numbers of words to narrate as accurately as possible the appearance of regular and irregular topographies; the layout and scenery of near and remote countries; and the distinctive behaviour of their civilized and savage inhabitants. All these details had to be presented through words alone, with no pictures, maps or diagrams, to an audience living in an environment utterly different from that in the surveyed region. This branch of ancient geography endowed medieval geographical writing with many of its characteristics.[66]

---

[66] Lozovsky (2000); Merrills (2005).

2.3 TRAVELOGUES AND CURIOSITIES

We have seen that geographical and ethnographic ideas as well as facts were integrated into early myths and were a significant part of the poetry of all periods. Simultaneously, the historiographic tradition from its very beginning absorbed and transmitted geographical information as part of its broad approach to the understanding of human existence in the world. All these channels of information were linked with a direct, practical acquaintance to regions around the world.[67] But such impressions were also transmitted in independent records of actual voyages. The section that follows does not offer a comprehensive study of travel in antiquity in all its aspects (i.e., extent, means, goals). Instead, it attempts to assess the connections between the physical presence of Greeks and Romans in different regions in the world, and the written transmission of their impressions. Encounters with foreign places and peoples aroused curiosity and amazement, and supplied fresh details for a set of texts that dealt with unusual or marvellous phenomena. The theme of travel thus connects to a growing interest in paradoxes and *mirabilia* (wonder tales).

The Greek myths described a number of heroic voyages by mythic travellers: the maddened Dionysus wandered throughout Asia and particularly India; Heracles visited the edges of the world while performing his labours; the Argonauts' quest for the Golden Fleece took them through considerable portions of eastern Europe; and Odysseus passed through much of the Mediterranean on his way from Troy to Ithaca. These were all legendary journeys that involved amazing experiences, and whose geographical background reflected the realities of their respective epochs (2.1). Actual expeditions of exploration, driven by both practical needs and genuine curiosity, were also carried out, and produced their own characteristic kind of recorded data.[68] Such journeys too inflamed the audience's imagination and served what seems to have been the taste of a wide popular readership. But from a modern critical point of view, the records of historical travels stand on a firmer factual ground than do myths. In antiquity, these reports included three principal types of documentation: *periploi, itineraria* and elaborate descriptions of travel experiences, and all three connect to the emergence of popular compilations of wonder tales and curiosities.

---

[67] Cary (1949).
[68] For general surveys of travel in antiquity, see Hyde (1947); Wheeler (1954), 119–207; Casson (1971); (1974); (1989), 11–44; (1994); Ellis and Kidner (2004); Roller (2006).

As travel for practical purposes, mainly commercial and military, became routine in the Archaic period and later in the Greek world, the need for accurate, reliable information based on the knowledge of experienced sailors increased (chapter 5). In all likelihood, oral advice was commonly shared, but written information was also offered when a combination of acquired knowledge and the need for information produced *periploi* (1.2).

The surviving specimens of the genre all focus on a specific maritime unit appropriate to the geographical horizons of the time: the Mediterranean or Inner Sea; the coasts of the Atlantic Ocean or Outer Sea; the Black Sea or Euxine;[69] and the southern seas (the Red Sea, the Persian Gulf and the Indian Ocean, sometimes referred to collectively as the Erythraean or 'Red' Sea). The earliest known *periplous* belongs to the sixth century BCE and is ascribed to a Greek from Massalia (Marseille).[70] The author's name is lost, but portions of his work served as the source for Avienus' *Ora Maritima* (fourth century CE). The *periplous* apparently described the coast at least from Massalia to Tartessus, possibly reflecting a commercial trip. Further evidence for the significance of the port of Massalia is a report of a certain Euthymenes based there, who in the sixth century BCE explored the west coast of Africa and offered (perhaps in writing) some odd and erroneous geographical insights:

> I have been on a voyage in the Atlantic. The Nile flows from there, and in greater volume as long as the Etesian winds are blowing in season, for at that time the sea is hurled out of itself inland by the pressure of the winds. When the winds subside, the sea is quiet and the descent of the Nile is correspondingly less forceful. Moreover, the taste of the sea is fresh and its animals are like the ones in the Nile. (Seneca, *QNat.* 4.2.22)

Euthymenes concluded that the Nile in Egypt was connected with the river he saw on the Atlantic, although this was in fact most likely the mouth of the Senegal River.

As knowledge of the Mediterranean gradually increased, voyages of exploration were launched to further regions. These journeys aimed at exploring unknown regions and gathering useful information. They too produced written reports, sometimes called *periploi*, although in some cases such reports contained additional descriptive detail and

---

[69] For its euphemistic definition as 'hospitable' (*euxeinos*), see Strabo 1.2.10; 7.3.6. On the multi-faceted significance of the Mediterranean, see Cary (1949), 1–36; Horden and Purcell (2000); Abulafia (2011).

[70] Earlier, Aristeas of Proconnesus recorded his travels in a poem (2.1).

occasionally emphasized the personal and emotional perspective of their authors, or offered exotic or exaggerated details. Even if they contained inaccurate or marvellous information, which reduced their reliability and thus their practical utility, such *periploi* still offered some information about general conditions in otherwise unknown regions. Trips of this sort often aspired to circumnavigate continents, to explore remote regions in order to discover shorter routes to other countries, to find new land for colonization, or to conquer foreign territory. Kings therefore often sponsored such expeditions: they could support them financially, and they had aspirations to expand their realms. Such involvement also enhanced a monarch's image even when actual achievements were limited.[71] In addition, simple curiosity and the drive for adventure must often have played a role.

The leading actors in the earliest voyages of exploration were neither Greeks nor Romans, but Egyptians, Phoenicians, Carthaginians and Persians. These nations were dominant political powers in the early history of the Mediterranean, and as such they controlled sea-routes and initiated the expansion of geographical knowledge. The explorations became known, on the other hand, almost exclusively through Greek and Roman written traditions. The importance of these voyages for the history of ancient geography is twofold: they significantly expanded the geographical horizons of their times, and the written documentation of such trips represents an important branch of descriptive geography.

According to Herodotus (4.42), King Necho II of Egypt (*c.* 600 BCE) was the first to prove that Africa was surrounded by water.[72] Necho initiated the digging of a canal from the Nile to the Arabian Gulf. He then sent a Phoenician expedition to sail from the Red Sea toward the south with the goal of circumnavigating Libya in a clockwise direction, by eventually entering the Straits of Gibraltar and returning to the Mediterranean coast of Egypt. The sailors accomplished the mission and reported that during their three-year journey they landed each autumn on African shores, staying there until spring and sowing and reaping grain. They also reported that, when they sailed around Africa, the sun stood to their right. Herodotus deemed this final comment incredible, but it may suggest the truth of the story, since for sailors sailing west in the southern hemisphere, the sun would in fact stand to the north of the vessel. Herodotus also supplies information about other expeditions of discovery:

---

[71] For the propaganda value of such endeavours, see Lloyd (1977) on Necho.
[72] For a sceptical view, see Lloyd (1977).

As to Asia, most of it was discovered by Darius ... desiring to know where the Indus issues into the sea, [he] sent ships manned by Scylax, a man of Caryanda, and others in whose word he trusted. These set out from the city of Caspatyrus [modern Multan, in Pakistan] ... and sailed down the river toward the east and the sunrise till they came to the sea. And voyaging over the sea westward, they came in the thirtieth month to that place whence the Egyptian king sent the Phoenicians mentioned above to sail round Libya. (4.44)

This Carian captain, Scylax, recorded his experience in writing (*c.* 519–516 BCE).[73] Two centuries after his adventures, another *periplous* was composed under the name Scylax, but this fourth-century BCE compilation of earlier information concentrated on the Mediterranean and the Black Sea,[74] and reflected Carthaginian domination of the sea and of harbours in the western Mediterranean.

Carthage, located at a central point on the northern shore of Africa (modern Tunisia), grew to become a dominant sea power. Political as well as economic interests motivated several Carthaginian notables to undertake expeditions outside the Mediterranean. Around 500 BCE, two expeditions left Carthage, sailing out through the Straits. One, led by Hanno, sailed south along the African coast. The other, led by Himilco, sailed north along the European coast. Some details of Hanno's expedition are known from a fourth-century BCE partial Greek translation of his records.[75] Hanno sailed with 60 ships in a bid to explore west Africa and establish new Punic colonies. The ships sailed only during the day and never lost sight of the coast. Hanno founded several Carthaginian settlements, passing along the shore of present-day Morocco from Tangier to Cape Juby directly east of the Canary Islands. He and his entourage saw volcanic activity both on the African coast and on the Canary Islands, and he encountered strange people:

There was another island full of savage people and most of them were women with hairy bodies; the translators called them 'Gorillas' ... after we killed them we took off their skin and brought the skins to Carthage. For we did not sail further because our food supply failed us. (sections 91–94, 98–100)

Himilco's four-month trip passed through Gades (modern Cadiz, in Spain) and continued along the Iberian coast to the Cassiterides, the 'Tin Islands' (the modern Isles of Scilly, or Cornwall in south-west Britain).

[73] *FGrHist* 709; Panchenko (1998); (2003).
[74] *GGM* 1.15–96; Lipinski (2004), 337–434.
[75] *GGM* 1.1–14; Picard (1982); Lipinski (2004), 435–475; Roller (2006), 129–132.

The information about his voyage is drawn from second-hand reports, since his original account and later translations were lost.[76]

The next known voyage of exploration was launched by the Persians, who attempted to sail around Africa. According to Herodotus (4.43), King Xerxes (reigned 486–465 BCE) punished Sataspes, a Persian noble who raped the daughter of one of his peers, by requiring him to undertake this mission. The voyage proceeded in a counter-clockwise direction from the Mediterranean coast of Egypt and through the Straits southward. Sataspes and his Egyptian crew managed to pass Cape Soloeis (modern Cape Spartel, in Morocco) and continued sailing south for many months. When Sataspes saw that the sea appeared endless, however, he returned, only to be crucified by Xerxes for failing to complete the mission. Although he did describe some encounters he had on the African coast, his reports were apparently oral, and there is no evidence of any written documentation.

In the fifth century BCE, *periploi* were composed describing various sections of coast. These were generally based on an accumulation of daily experiences by sailors rather than representing the result of a specific targeted mission. Avienus mentions several sources for his poem, including a set of such *periploi* originating in the fifth century BCE (*OM* 82 ff.): Damastes of Sigeum, who thought the Arabian Gulf was a lake;[77] Euctemon of Athens, who was interested primarily in astronomy, but also described regions in the western Mediterranean; Phileas of Athens, who regarded the Rhône as the border between Europe and Libya; and Bacoris of Rhodes, who composed a *periplous* of an unknown scope. At the beginning of the fourth century BCE, Ctesias of Cnidus wrote (in addition to his local histories of Persia and India) a treatise entitled, according to various reports, *Periodos, Periêgêsis* or *Periplous*, which surveyed Asia, Libya and Italy.[78] Although little of the original work survives, the genre was clearly flourishing at this time.

The conquests of Alexander the Great not only extended Greek knowledge of continental territory, but expanded potential maritime horizons as well. On Alexander's orders (Arr. *Ind.* 20.1–2), Nearchus of Crete was asked to make the journey from India to Susa by sea and to produce an accurate account of coasts, harbours, gulfs and towns. Nearchus and Onesicritus recorded Nearchus' journey down the Indus and through

---

[76] See mainly Plin. *HN* 2.169a; Avienus, *OM* 117–129, 380–389, 402–415.
[77] *FGrHist* 5.
[78] *FGrHist* 688 F 55–59; F 74 – *On Rivers*; F 73 – *On Mountains*.

the Persian Gulf to the Euphrates.[79] The report described the first visit of Greeks to Tylus (modern Bahrain):

All this was told to Alexander, partly by Archias, who was sent with a thirty-oared ship to explore the coastal route toward Arabia and who arrived at the island Tylus, but did not venture further. But Androsthenes was dispatched with another thirty-oared vessel, and sailed around part of the Arabian peninsula. But farthest of all those who were sent out advanced Hieron of Soli the steersman, who also received a thirty-oared ship from Alexander. For his sailing orders were to coast round the whole Arabian peninsula, till he reached the Arabian Gulf on the Egyptian side, near Heropolis. Yet he did not dare to advance further, though he had sailed round the greater part of Arabia; but he turned about, and reported to Alexander the size of the peninsula as vast and not far short of that of India, and that a projection ran far into the Ocean. (Arr. *Anab.* 7.20.7–8)

The expedition encountered extraordinary phenomena:

Nearchus states that when they left Cyiza [in modern Pakistan], about daybreak, they saw water being blown upward from the sea as it might be shot upward by the force of a waterspout. They were astonished and asked the pilots of the convoy what it might be and how it was caused. They replied that the whales as they roamed about the Ocean spout up the water to a great height. The sailors, however, were so startled that the oars fell from their hands. (Arr. *Ind.* 8.30.1–3)

At about the same time, a famous traveller whose reports were already controversial in antiquity sailed to the north Atlantic.[80] Pytheas of Massalia (*fl. c.* 310–306 BCE) recorded his impressions in *On the Ocean*. This was more than a *periplous*, since it also featured astronomical observations that served later scholars such as Hipparchus in their calculations of latitudes (3.3). Pytheas offered practical instructions for merchants sailing in the northern Ocean, including in regions never explored before his time. His sailing trip, which probably lasted at least two years, departed from Massalia, passed the Pillars to Gades, and from there proceeded north to Cape Ortegal (modern Ortigueira, in Spain), the Loire, the island of Uxisame (Ouessant, in France) and Belerium (Cape Cornwall). Pytheas was probably the first Greek to circumnavigate Britain and to describe its climate and inhabitants. Travelling even further north, he saw an island he named Thule (Iceland or the Shetlands[81]) and other islands abounding in amber. Because Pytheas had visited previously unknown regions and described unusual natural and human phenomena, some ancient authors questioned his reliability and called him a liar (Strabo 1.4.3). But a number

[79] Plin. *HN* 6.96–100; Brown (1949), 105–124; Pearson (1983).
[80] Roseman (1994); Cunliffe (2003); Roller (2006), 57–91.
[81] Wijsman (1998).

of details in his descriptions, including his observations of typical northern astronomical phenomena, show that he most likely sailed as far as the
Shetland Islands, possibly seeing the coast of Iceland from a distance.

In the Hellenistic age, local rulers or their agents were typically involved
in sea explorations. Ophelas (320–310 BCE) was a ruler of Cyrene who composed a *periplous* of the Atlantic coast of Africa (Strabo 17.3.3). Patrocles,
an admiral of Seleucus I, conducted a *c.* 284 BCE voyage of exploration
in the Caspian Sea,[82] while Demodamas, a military commander under
Seleucus and Antiochus, crossed the Jaxartes (Plin. *HN* 6.49). The maritime space between Africa and India also interested the ancients, most
likely because routes to the east were essential for commerce in spices and
incense.[83] Sponsored by the Ptolemies, Agatharchides of Cnidus (200–140
BCE) composed a *periplous* of the Erythraean Sea, which included in its
survey Ptolemaic activity in the Red Sea, geographical conditions in the
upper Nile Valley, and ethnic patterns on the African coast of the Red
Sea and the coast of Arabia.[84]

Ptolemy VIII (reigned 145–116 BCE) was motivated by an unusual event
to send an expedition to explore the route between India and Egypt: an
Indian sailor was found alone and half-dead on a ship in the Arabian Gulf,
and was brought to the king. Ptolemy responded by sending Eudoxus of
Cyzicus on a mission of exploration.[85] On his return to Egypt, Eudoxus
drifted south of Ethiopia, where he found a horse-shaped wooden prow
of a ship from Gades that had sailed beyond the Lixus River (modern
Loukkos, in Morocco) but never returned. He concluded that it was
possible to circumnavigate Africa and attempted the voyage, departing
from Cyzicus with a large entourage. The ship sank, and Eudoxus made
a second attempt but never returned. Eudoxus' endeavours thus involved
the route from Egypt to India, where he probably followed the monsoon
and not the coast, and the route around Africa from west to east.

Around 100 BCE, another Hellenistic scholar based in Asia Minor
composed a descriptive geographical work. Artemidorus of Ephesus
described the entire world in eleven books preserved through an abstract
made about five centuries later by Marcianus of Heraclea.[86] Artemidorus'
work followed the general outline of a *periplous*, included calculations of
topographical measurements, and was divided into three sections corresponding to the three continents. Artemidorus relied on his own travels

---

[82] *FGrHist* 712 F 1–8; Plin *HN* 6.58.
[83] Rougé (1988). [84] Burstein (1989).
[85] Strabo 2.3.4; Thiel (1966). [86] *GGM* 1.574–576.

as well as the writings of Agatharchides (2.3), Megasthenes and the historians of Alexander of Macedon. His importance lies in his role as a basic source of information for later geographers, but considerable interest was recently aroused by the discovery of a three-metre-long papyrus roll associated with his name.[87] Some scholars have suggested that this was part of Artemidorus' lost work and that the papyrus contains excerpts of Artemidorus' general remarks on geography as a branch of philosophy and the beginning of his survey of Iberia. Others reject the identification, mainly on linguistic grounds. Most important, the papyrus contains drawings, mostly of animals and body organs, but perhaps also a sketch of a river delta. If so, this would be the earliest remains of a map on papyrus (chapter 4).

A few years later, Xenophon of Lampsacus (100–60 BCE) produced a *periplous* of the coast of northern and western Europe, probably referring to Scandinavia (Balcia):

Xenophon of Lampsacus reports that at a distance of three days' sail from the Scythian coast there is an island of enormous size called Balcia; Pytheas gives its name as Basilia. Also some islands called Oeonae are reported, the inhabitants of which live on birds' eggs and oats, and others on which people are born with horses' feet, which give them their Greek name, Hippopodes. There are others called the Panotii ['all-ears'] Islands, in which the natives have very large ears covering the whole of their bodies, which are otherwise left naked. (Plin. *HN* 4.95)

Although many Hellenistic *periploi* dealt with particularly remote areas, interest in nearer seas did not fade. In the first century BCE, Menippus of Pergamum composed a *periplous* of the inner sea (the Mediterranean) in at least three books and perhaps a fourth on the Black Sea.[88] These are known through abstracts made in the late fourth century CE by Marcianus of Heraclea. The work's emphasis on sailing is apparent from its allusion to coasts, harbours and the distances between coastal points.

Another *periplous*, attributed to an unidentified Greek from Roman Egypt, is the *Periplus Maris Erythraei*, dated to the mid-first century CE.[89] The text is based on the author's personal experience and deals with two major trading routes, both of which rely on the south-west and north-east monsoons: (1) the African route from the Egyptian ports of the Red Sea through its southern straits to the Gulf of Aden and along the eastern

---

[87] Canfora (2007); Gallazzi *et al.* (2008); Brodersen and Elsner (2009).
[88] *GGM* 1.563–573; Diller (1952), 147–164.
[89] Casson (1989), 283–291.

coast of Africa to the region of modern Tanzania; and (2) the Arabian/ Indian route from the Egyptian ports of the Red Sea through its southern straits, either along the southern coast of Arabia to north-west India, or through the open waters of the Indian Ocean to south-west India. This *periplous* emphasizes information useful to traders, such as easily accessible harbours, interesting commodities and the degree of friendliness of the local inhabitants. Various other details of local history, physics, botany and ethnography are provided, but the language is both technical and yet simple, since the goal of the document appears to be practical rather than intellectual.

A century later, Arrian (120–170 CE) offered a record of trade routes along the coasts of the Black Sea.[90] This *periplous* is formulated as a letter to Hadrian, intended to offer practical information about the regions around the Black Sea. Arrian's position as a governor of Cappadocia, as well as his use of earlier sources, enabled him to supply details about distances and safe harbours in his survey of the coast from Trapezus to Sebastopolis. But there is a difference in the level of detail and information between the more accurate section concerning the south and east side of the sea, as opposed to that concerning its northern coast.

Finally, Marcianus of Heraclea (*c.* 400 CE) is known for his summaries of geographical treatises of earlier authors such as Artemidorus (*GGM* 1.574–576) and Menippus. But he also produced his own *Periplous of the Outer Sea*, which is almost entirely preserved (*GGM* 1.515–562). The first book describes the coasts of the Arabian Gulf and the Indian Ocean, including the Persian Gulf as far as the Gulf of the Sinae (probably the Gulf of Thailand). The second book describes the coasts of the Atlantic Ocean from Spain to Britain.

This survey of the historical circumstances of tours of maritime exploration and their written records as *periploi* makes it clear that Greeks dominated this domain even in the time of the Roman Empire (Mennipus, Arrian, Marcianus). Relatively few Romans extended the scope of maritime knowledge, although one might cite Agricola's British achievements as recorded by Tacitus, or Strabo's reference to a certain Publius Crassus, who visited the Cassiterides (Tin Islands) and 'laid abundant information before all who wished to traffic over this sea, albeit a wider sea than that which separates Britain from the continent' (3.5.11).

Our discussion up to this point has been concerned with naval journeys and the written logs they produced. But throughout antiquity people

[90] *GGM* 1.370–401; Marenghi (1958); Stadter (1980), 32–41; Silberman (1993); (1995).

travelled on land as well, and accounts of these experiences were sometimes recorded in writing. In the first century BCE, Isidorus of Charax produced a systematic account of the caravan trail from Zeugma to India, for the benefit of merchants.[91] In his *Stathmoi Parthikoi*, Isidorus gave names of stations, their order on the route and the distances between them. He also integrated some exotic descriptive details, such as an account of the pearl fisheries in the Persian Gulf.

A similarly systematic written approach to land-routes was undertaken by the Romans. As the Empire expanded, the administrative centre in Rome had to be able to connect efficiently with all its subject territories. Gradually an elaborate road system was created for official use (*cursus publicus*).[92] But others travelled by land as well: soldiers; citizens coming to Rome to vote in assemblies; merchants; and even tourists. Only a few individuals in this period could afford the time and money needed to engage in tourism. Historians, for example, and their counterparts who produced geographical treatises, often brag about the extent of their travels, particularly because autopsy was considered the best evidence. Egypt, for example, became a 'must' on the itinerary list of historians and other intellectuals.[93]

Relying on the efficient and expanding system of imperial roads throughout the empire, written records of land-routes and distances were produced to ease the journeys of travellers. Such *itineraria*, as they were called, were a uniquely Roman phenomenon.[94] An *itinerarium adnotatum* ('annotated') offered a list of place-names and the distances between them. In this way, a traveller could discover where to go and the distance to his destination, which could be translated into the duration of a march. This style of presentation enabled progress only along an existing linear route between two points, and offered no alternative routes or bypasses. Distances between points 'as the crow flies' were meaningless in antiquity, and the focus was on the best, most convenient and shortest way to reach a place. An *itinerarium pictum* probably translated spatial and toponymic information into graphic form, by depicting routes, sites and the distances between them. The format was in fact a sort of general orienteering map, but apparently not to scale (chapter 4).

---

[91] *GGM* 1.244–256; *FGrHist* 781; Schoff (1914); Chaumont (1984).
[92] Casson (1974), 163–175; Davies (1998).
[93] See for instance Diod. Sic. 1.69.3–4; 1.96.1–2; Ball (1942); Montiglio (2000); (2006).
[94] Brodersen (2001); Salway (2001) for late texts, see Geyer *et al.* (1965). See also the demonstration of their use in Isaac (1996).

Several *itineraria adnotata* are known, all written at the height of the Roman Empire. The Antonine Itinerary (third century CE) is a collection of provincial itineraries covering the entire Empire and arranged according to region.[95] It starts at the Pillars of Heracles, moving around the Mediterranean from northern Africa to Europe. Not all regions enjoyed the same level of detailed gazetteer. Frequently the text offered records of clusters of roads and sites along them as they connected central points such as Rome, Milan and London. Elsewhere, as for islands, it offered disconnected independent units. The collection also included maritime itineraries with lists of coastal points (*periploi*).

Other itineraries dealt with journeys to specific destinations. Theophanes of Hermopolis recorded *c*. 320 CE an account of his travel to and from Antioch.[96] Although written in Greek, this *itinerarium* gives distances in miles and reflects the fourth-century Roman network of roads. The anonymous Bordeaux Itinerary (*Itinerarium Burdigalense* or *Itinerarium Hierosolymitanum*), dated to 333 CE, records a pilgrimage 'from Bordeaux to Jerusalem, and from Heraclea to Milan through Valona and Rome',[97] indicating, in intervals reckoned in the Gallic *leuga* (2,200 m.), way-stations where horses could be changed (*mutationes*), inns (*mansiones*), cities (*civitates*) and occasional geographical features. This is its opening section:

The city of Burdigala [Bordeaux], which the river Garonna [Garonne] flows through, and through which the Ocean enters and withdraws for about 100 leugae; station in Stomata 7 leugae; station in Sirio 9 leugae; the city of Vasata 9 leugae; station in three trees 5 leugae … The total from Bordeaux to Arelate [Arles] 372 miles, 30 stations, 11 inns … the city of Dea Vocontiorum [Luc] 16 miles; inn in Lucus 12 miles; station in Vologatis 9 miles … from there Mount Gaura ascends … inn in Catorigas 12 miles; inn in Ebreduno 16 miles; from there start the Cottiae Alps. (550–555)

Itineraria recorded information on routes that were part of the regular imperial road system, even in remote provinces. There are also a few indications, however, that the Romans launched expeditions on land for the sake of exploration, although these are almost always connected with political ends of conquest or diplomacy. Aelius Gallus, the Roman prefect of Egypt in 26–24 BCE:

was sent by Augustus Caesar to explore the tribes and the places not only in Arabia but also in Ethiopia … but he was deceived by the Nabataean

[95] Salway (2001), esp. 39–43; Talbert (2007).
[96] Matthews (2006).   [97] Bowman (1998).

administrator Syllaeus who ... pointed out neither a safe voyage along the coast nor a safe journey by land, misguiding him through places that had no roads and by circuitous routes and through regions destitute of everything. (Strabo 16.4.22–23)

Gallus combined ships and infantry on his expedition, but failed in his mission and lost men to the region's extreme topographic and climatic conditions: the heat afflicted the soldiers with fatigue, hunger and thirst; many fell ill with scurvy; they were forced to depend on local guides who betrayed them and caused the army further losses.

Another territory explored by land, possibly on camels, was the Sahara,[98] which was crossed by several Romans, among them L. Cornelius Balbus, who in 19 BCE defeated the Saharan tribe of the Garamantes:

After these a long range stretches from east to west, which our people from its nature call the Black Mountain ... beyond this mountain range is the desert, and then a town of the Garamantes called Thelgae, and also Debris, near which there is a spring of which the water is boiling hot from midday to midnight and then freezing cold for the same number of hours until midday, and Garama, the celebrated capital of the Garamantes; all of which places have been subdued by the arms of Rome, being conquered by Cornelius Balbus, who was given a triumph ... our writers have handed down the names of the towns mentioned above as having been taken by him, and have stated that in his own triumphal procession beside Cydamus and Garama were carried the names and images of all the other races and cities, which went in this order: the town of Tabudium, the Niteris tribe, the town of Milgis Gemella, the tribe or town of Bubeium, the tribe of the Enipi, the town of Thuben, the mountain known as Black Mountain, the towns called Nitibrum and Rapsa, the Viscera tribe, the town of Decri, the river Nathabur, the town of Thapsagum, the Tamiagi tribe, the town of Boin, the town of Pege, the river Dasibari; then a series of towns, Baracum, Buluba, Alasit, Galsa, Balla, Maxalla, Cizania; and Mount Gyri. (Plin. *HN* 5.35–37)

Finally, the Romans reached as far as China, establishing contacts with the local *Seres*.[99] These 'silk people' (*sericus* meaning 'silken') 'are of inoffensive manners, but, bearing a strong resemblance to all savage nations, they shun all intercourse with the rest of mankind, and await the approach of those who wish to traffic with them' (Plin. *HN* 6.54). Despite this unfavourable impression, the Romans traded with the Chinese and had reciprocal contacts with the court there as early as the time of Augustus:

---

[98] Desanges (1964); Mauny (2002). Earlier knowledge already in Herodotus 2.181–185, and see Carpenter (1956).
[99] Thorley (1971); Leslie and Gardiner (1996); Hill (2009).

Now that all the races of the west and south were subjugated, and also the races of the north, those at least between the Rhine and the Danube, and of the east between the Cyrus and the Euphrates, the other nations too, who were not under the rule of the Empire, yet felt the greatness of Rome and revered its people as the conqueror of the world. For the Scythians and the Sarmatians sent ambassadors seeking friendship; the Seres too and the Indians, who live immediately beneath the sun, though they brought elephants among their gifts as well as precious stones and pearls, regarded their long journey, in the accomplishment of which they had spent four years, as the greatest tribute which they rendered; and indeed their complexion proved that they came from beneath another sky. (Florus 2.34.61–62)

As a part of the tradition of recorded travels, though using a more detailed descriptive style, Pausanias of Magnesia in Asia Minor produced *c.* 180 CE his *Periegesis Hellados* (*Description of Greece*), which presented his wide-ranging travels during 20 years, particularly in mainland Greece.[100] While moving between *poleis* and sanctuaries on the mainland, Pausanias made meticulous lists of what he saw, including details of local artefacts, traditions and cults. Before or after these visits, he studied earlier works in search of information on the sites, particularly their history and mythic traditions. He then incorporated that information into his lists. The result is not a simple, naïve traveller's record, but a work with significant literary aspirations, influenced by and responding to, specific intellectual Hellenic traditions.

Pausanias wanted to instruct prospective tourists, and he accordingly emphasized the point of view of a traveller more than that of a geographer, noting works of art and monuments in particular:

These are the most remarkable sights that meet a man who goes over the Altis [at Olympia] according to the instructions I have given. But if you go to the right from the Leonidaeum to the great altar [of Zeus], you will come across the following notable objects. (6.17.1)

The survey, which is divided into ten detailed books, each devoted to a region within Greece, nonetheless also offers glimpses of topographical features hinting at a background *periplous*, such as: 'Of the Greek islands, Aegina is the most difficult of access, for it is surrounded by sunken rocks and reefs which rise up' (2.29.6).

The main structuring principle of Pausanias' work was his travels, and numerous sections of his narrative represent a sort of *itinerarium* supplying details on routes from one site to another. But these features

[100] Habicht (1985); Arafat (1996); Elsner (2001); Pretzler (2004); (2005); (2007); Hutton (2005).

seem to be merely the framework for the main body of the composition, which is a broad survey of local art and history. Pausanias probably travelled on foot, and he visited many sites he had come to know
from earlier texts as important and significant. Indeed, he visited some
of them more than once. His trips can thus be interpreted as a sort
of intellectual pilgrimage resulting from a deliberate travel schedule,
although not necessarily with a precise overall goal. The result is an
inclusive work that contains numerous details that reflect its author's
design and, most important for the present discussion, the longest and
most detailed narrative from classical antiquity of one individual's experiences as a traveller.

Travel by land or sea thus gradually grew easier through the existence
of various kinds of compiled and recorded information. At the same time,
travel stories were (and remain) imbued with exaggerations based on awe
and excitement at foreign places and unusual experiences. Encounters with
exotic countries and strange people aroused curiosity in both travellers
and the public at home, a phenomenon which peaked in the Hellenistic
era, probably as a result of the adventures of Alexander, and produced a
lively taste for remarkable phenomena.

In the third century BCE, a new literary phenomenon emerged: collections of marvellous stories excerpted from works of history, geography and
science.[101] Authors compiled wonder tales (*thaumata* in Greek, *mirabilia*
in Latin), sometimes defined as *paradoxa*, that is, phenomena contrary to
human expectation (*doxa*). These compilations recorded unexpected features in the natural world (strange animals, extraordinary plants, unusual
rivers or springs) or marvellous details of human life (e.g., irregular physi-
ology or strange social habits). But they always concerned the real world.

The relationship between paradoxography and geography was a close
one: the wonders in the compilations were often taken from geographical
works, both descriptive and scientific, and some of these works accordingly preserve ancient geographical information. Moreover, descriptions of countries and regions, particularly unknown ones, necessarily
involved strange and unusual details, which were the essence of *thaumata*
and *mirabilia*. Some of these compilations were arranged geographically. Callimachus, considered the father of the paradoxographical tradition, composed a collection of world marvels arranged, as far as we can

---

[101] For the texts, see Giannini (1966). For discussion, see Jacob (1983); Schepens and Delcroix
(1996) pp. 373–409 for the Hellenistic period (Schepens), pp. 410–452 for the Roman period,
(Delcroix); Hardie (2009).

tell, according to six geographical regions: central and north Greece, the Peloponnese, Thrace, Italy, Libya and Asia.[102]

The 'paradoxographers' intended their collections to include only phenomena that were observed and reported, since these would otherwise be regarded not as wonders but as fantasies. Their collections were therefore mostly based on existing works or, less often, on the personal experiences of the authors, and it was important to name the source for each fact (contrast the lack of references in, for example, historiography). Tales were arranged systematically, either in verse or in prose, generally according to four principles: geographical (e.g., 'Marvels in India'), thematic (e.g., zoological *paradoxa*), alphabetical and bibliographic (by the source consulted).

Geographical and ethnographic oddities were a standard component in early geographical writing and were common throughout antiquity, for example in Herodotus, Aristotle and Ctesias. Some themes persisted as natural mysteries or exceptional phenomena.[103] One such mystery, which perplexed numerous authors, was the question of the source of the Nile and the reason for its annual inundation. This was deemed a mystery because the river swelled seasonally with no visible cause. Several explanations (summed up by Mela 1.53) were offered: melting snow from the Ethiopian mountains; the changing seasonal distance from the sun which, when nearer, dried up part of the river; the Etesian winds pushing rain clouds over the source of the river; and adverse winds blocking the flow of the water.[104] Descriptions of strange nations of extraordinary appearance or unusual habits were also common in paradoxographies; examples include the gorillas in Africa (Hanno), the dog-headed people (*Cynocephaloi*) and the Sciapodes in India (Ctesias and Megasthenes), and the fish-eaters and turtle-eaters on the coast of the Red Sea (Strabo).

Like its Hellenistic predecessor, Roman paradoxography targeted intellectuals looking for excerpts to use in other literary works, as well as a wider public interested in natural phenomena and human customs in remote and unknown regions.[105] But the Roman context and atmosphere at the height of the Empire added a particular interest in monstrosities and deformities of nature:

---

[102] Giannini (1966), 15–20.
[103] For instance, floating rocks and islands; see Nishimura-Jensen (2000).
[104] Euthymenes of Massalia, as noted, thought the Nile's source was a river (the Senegal) in west Africa, *FGrHist* 647 F 1.5.
[105] Evans (1999).

The Blemyes lack heads; their faces are in their chests. (Mela 1.48)[106]

This [the satyr] is an extremely swift animal, sometimes going on all fours, sometimes standing upright like human beings. (Plin. *HN* 7.24)

The emperors used *mirabilia* of farther regions as a symbol of their domination. In such contexts, the edges of the earth, for example India and northern Europe, were prominent as regions rich in deformities and natural oddities. Africa in particular was considered a region of confusion, inhabited by monstrous animals and peoples.

Iulius Solinus (fl. 230–240 CE) composed a *Collectanea Rerum Memorabilium* – a collection of geographical information borrowed mainly from Mela and Pliny. He condensed Pliny's text to a manageable size (an important contribution as such) and, after offering a brief survey of Roman history from its foundation, he began his description of the world with Italy, indicating his own ideological emphases. Solinus was particularly fond of *mirabilia*, that is, unusual human and natural phenomena, but also offered a mode of description which was different from that of his predecessors. While Mela and Pliny still adhered to the linear mode based on coastlines as guide-lines (the *periplous* model), Solinus tended to describe *areas*, as he introduced the concept of terrestrial *plaga* ('region' or 'zone') to define spatial units on the earth. He enhanced this regional model by indicating neighbouring regions for each area and by adding directions. And, as a result of this approach, he innovated the use of the terms 'Mediterranean' and 'Orient' to roughly indicate the regions we tag to this day with these titles.[107] This new approach is perhaps a reflection of cartographic notions which were shaped in Solinus' age (chapter 4). All this gave his work a unique tone and gained a wide readership in the Middle Ages; at least 350 manuscripts survive.

This review of ancient travel records and collections of wonders suggests that there was no uniform way of perceiving movement or space. Both travelogues and paradoxography were derived from encounters with foreign countries, and both have a part to play in modern reconstructions of early geographical knowledge and perceptions. Their approaches are none the less quite different. In general, in travel descriptions, whether based on land or sea journeys, the linear physical progress of the traveller determined the order of description. Beyond this, the choice of method of survey and the emphases within it were derived from the experience

---

[106] Mela's quotations are based on the translation by Romer (1998).
[107] Brodersen (2011).

of the author, his literary tendencies and his scholarly background. Paradoxographies, on the other hand, emphasized natural phenomena with geographical relevance, not an orderly spatial or linear description of foreign places. What is common to all works discussed in this section is their assimilation of newly discovered regions and ground-breaking explorations.

Early travels were mainly maritime and involved reaching new horizons on the remotest parts of the three continents, including the southern coast of Africa, the northern coasts of Europe, and the Indian Ocean. The Greeks and Romans eventually learned of islands beyond the immediate outline of the three continents: Britain, Scandinavia, Iceland, the Canary Islands and Sri Lanka.[108] These expansions of nautical horizons were complemented by a gradual growth in land travel through previously unexplored regions such as the Sahara, the Punjab and China. The geographical reach of the classical world thus extended (using modern terminology) from Iceland to China, and from north of the Caspian Sea to Zanzibar and Guinea.

---

[108] Weerakkody (1997).

CHAPTER 3

Mathematical geography

3.1 SHAPES AND SIZES

Our mental image of the world is always based on a combination of actual geographical knowledge and imagination, that is, on a mix of directly experienced and abstractly conceived space. In antiquity, when remote regions were still inaccessible, legendary elements played a larger role. But after travel and conquest increased direct acquaintance with distant frontiers, solid facts based on autopsy began to support more accurate reports and theories.

Early notions of the world occasionally combined myths with real facts derived from experience. At the same time, in the Archaic period (seventh–sixth centuries BCE) a rationalistic approach to understanding the universe and the world emerged. This tendency sought scientific explanations based on sensory assessment and logical inference, and produced the mathematical branch of geographical discussion. This approach continued to be practised thereafter throughout antiquity alongside the descriptive one. As was argued in chapter 2, the descriptive approach did not refrain from considering marvellous and paradoxical situations in a way contradictory to scientific thinking. But the factual foundation of both branches solidified with the growth in direct knowledge of remote regions.

As noted earlier, the descriptive branch of ancient geography used words, mostly drawn from direct experience, to convey geographical facts and ideas. Because words were its means, descriptions had to be elaborated, often at length, to communicate the nature of the regions in question and how individual landscapes looked. Scientific or mathematical geography used different methodologies and were probably aimed at a different readership. But it engaged with similar issues, primarily the discussion of local features with an emphasis on explaining natural phenomena. This 'scientific' approach did not apply science in the modern sense, that is, a systematic and controlled methodology based on observations and experimentation and resulting in an organized body of knowledge. In this sense classical geography was never 'scientific'. It did, however, exploit mathematical methods and premises based on sensory perception, and used logical argumentation to combine these conclusions into coherent theories regarding the shape and size of the world and its component parts: continents, regions, seas and rivers. It employed methods for measuring geographical features, such as perimeters and heights, and offered definitions of general rules and explanations of natural phenomena such as inundations, tides, volcanic eruptions and ethnic diversity. Mathematical (or 'scientific' henceforth) geography thus used numbers and calculation to achieve its goals, whereas the cartographic branch, which relied on scientific conclusions, used graphic means to express its observations (chapter 4).

Early Greek cosmology discussed the material composition of the universe as a whole, including the part of the earth on which mankind resides. The primary Homeric concept of the world was as a flat disk, including a circular portion of land surrounded by the Ocean, which was unlimited and therefore undefined and frightening. The Presocratic philosophers discussed the material nature of the earth, and their ideas were the point of departure for the discussions of scientific geography. Anaximander of Miletus (*c.* 580–545 BCE) and Anaxagoras of Clazomenae (*c.* 480–428 BCE) understood the world to be a concave circle.[1] But Pythagoras (*c.* 570–495 BCE) and Parmenides of Elea (*c.* 520–450 BCE) claimed, on theoretical grounds alone, that the earth must be spherical, and this became a basic datum of Greek cosmology thereafter.[2] Herodotus, on the other hand, retains the idea of the world as a flat disk, as is apparent from his comment that the heat in India was at its peak in the morning but decreased toward evening (Hdt. 3.104). India was traditionally situated at the eastern edge of the inhabited world, and it was therefore assumed that the sun was closest to the *oikoumenê* in the east in the morning, and gradually went further west while the air was cooling down. Even in Aristotle's time the consensus was incomplete:

There is just as much disagreement about the shape of the earth. Some think it is spherical, others that it is flat and shaped like a drum. These latter adduce as evidence the fact that the sun at its setting and rising shows a straight instead of a curved line where it is cut off from view by the horizon, whereas, were the

---

[1] Panchenko (1997).
[2] Solmsen (1960); Heidel (1976); Rescher (2005).

earth spherical, the line of section would necessarily be curved. (*Cael.* 2.13, 293b34–294a4)

But elsewhere the senses suggested a different conclusion:

We see that throughout the *oikoumenê*, the horizon always changes as we move, which indicates that we live on the convex surface of a sphere. (*Mete.* 365a30–32)

At the beginning of the third century BCE, Epicurus returned to the ideas of Anaximenes, who claimed that the sun set behind remote, high mountains situated at the edge of the flat earth. This was the background for Dicaearchus of Messana's extended re-discussion of the spherical shape of the earth, which included astronomical evidence offered to show that different stars were visible from various southern or northern points on the earth.[3] After that, it was generally recognized that the earth was a globe.

Once the shape of the world was more or less defined and accepted, efforts were made to assess its size, first by general estimation and then by precise calculation.[4] For this purpose, defined standards for measuring length and distance were needed. How, then, were distances between points, and eventually large spatial intervals, measured? Writers using travel experience described distance primarily in terms of time, indicating the length of a journey from one place to another. Such definitions were inaccurate and occasionally exaggerated, as for example Nestor's comment that the sea extending to Africa was so vast that it took birds a year to fly there (*Od.* 3.321). But such indications could at least offer the appearance of precision: the voyage to the island of Pharos off the coast of Egypt was said to require one complete day of sailing (*Od.* 4.354–357). These methods of estimation prevailed also in later and supposedly more accurate records, for example in Herodotus: 'from here [Cilicia] it is a straight five days' journey for an unburdened man to Sinope on the Black Sea' (2.34). Later, Eratosthenes of Cyrene, who successfully calculated the circumference of the earth (see below), estimated the distance from Alexandria to Syene in Egypt by the time it took a caravan of camels to travel between the two points. All such judgements were necessarily estimates, because they were subjective and depended on weather conditions; the size of the vessel and number of sailors (if the voyage was by sea); or the means of transport (if the journey was by land), whether by foot, horseback or mule-cart.

---

[3] Heidel (1976), 113–121; Keyser (2001), 361–365.
[4] Diller (1949); Evans (1998), 63–66; Lewis (2001), 143–156.

There was a fundamental difference between measuring shorter distances and longer ones. Although short distances could be measured by pacing (specialists were called *bematistae*), it was much more difficult to measure longer ones, especially when the route between two points was indirect or non-existent, for example, when an attempt was made to calculate the distance between Susa and Rome, or the size of large geographical units. Longer distances were therefore generally calculated by adding shorter intervals together rather than by pacing, and this naturally produced only approximate numbers.

Pacers made actual measurements by counting steps, and then calculated distance on that basis. The Greek *stadion* consisted of 600 Greek feet.[5] The length of a foot varied at different times and places in Greece. Modern interpretation of ancient distances therefore depends on the specific choice of foot-length. But to give a rough idea of the approximate length of the *stadion*: on the basis of the Attic foot – 29.6 centimetres – it was equal to about 178 metres. The Romans adapted the Greek system, by using paces (*passus*) and measuring distances in units of 1,000 paces (*milia passuum*).[6] A Roman 'mile' consisted of 5,000 Roman feet of 29.6 centimetres, and was thus equal to about 1,480 metres. The standard conversion rate between Greek and Roman standards was eight *stadia* to the mile (Strabo 7.7.4). Herodotus demonstrated a transitional phase between the older method and the more accurate one, by indicating that a one-day journey equalled 150 *stadia* (Hdt. 5.53).

Ancient assessments of the shape and size of the world, both conceptually and mathematically, depended fundamentally on how the word 'world' was interpreted. The earth might be understood as a body consisting of both land and water, or as the land alone, which in antiquity was synonymous with the inhabited world (*oikoumenê*). A basic precondition for assessing any object's size and shape is defining its borders or the limits of the specific units being measured. General notions about the layout of the world thus affected attempts to calculate its size precisely.[7] Aristotle, for example, raised the possibility that the Atlantic Ocean connected with the Indian Ocean, and that the distance between the two was not particularly large:

[5] See the comprehensive discussion in Pothecary (1995).
[6] Herodotus also mentions the Egyptian *schoenus* and the Persian *parasang* (2.6, 5.53), while *leugae* were used in some Roman itineraries.
[7] Evans (1998), 63–66.

They produce also in support of their contention the fact that elephants are a species found at the extremities of both lands, arguing that this phenomenon at the
extremes is due to communication between the two. Mathematicians who try to
calculate the circumference put it at 400,000 *stadia*. From these arguments we
must conclude not only that the earth's mass is spherical, but also that it is not
large in comparison with the size of the other stars. (*Cael.* 2.14, 298a13–b20)

Unlike Plato's concept of an unlimited Ocean, as implied in his Atlantis
legend (see below), Aristotle thought of a smaller globe including a smaller
Atlantic Ocean. He offered the figure of 400,000 *stadia* (about 74,000
kilometres) for the circumference of the world, without supplying his
method of calculation. A few years later, in about 305 BCE, Aristotle's student Dicaearchus, whose research was sponsored by the Hellenistic kings
Lysimachus and Ptolemy I, estimated the circumference of the earth at
300,000 *stadia* (55,500 kilometres).[8] Archimedes (*c.* 287–212 BCE) suggested 3,000,000 (!) *stadia*,[9] but this was merely a conjecture and a working hypothesis in the context of research intended to express extremely
large numbers.

The first recorded systematic attempt to calculate the circumference
of the spherical earth was made by Eratosthenes of Cyrene (*c.* 276–195
BCE).[10] Eratosthenes was the head of the library in Alexandria and a prolific and enthusiastic intellectual, who was involved in many branches
of knowledge, including poetry, astronomy and geography. He was also
most likely the first to use the word *geôgraphia* to denote a description of
the world. The details of his attempt to calculate the circumference of the
earth are reported by the astronomer Cleomedes in his second-century CE
treatise *On Orbits of the Celestial Bodies*:

About the size of the earth, the physicists, or natural philosophers, have held
different views, but those of Posidonius and Eratosthenes are preferable to the
rest. The latter shows the size of the earth by a geometrical method; the method
of Posidonius is simpler. Both lay down certain hypotheses, and by successive
inferences from the hypotheses, they arrive at their demonstrations. (1.10)[11]

In his lost work *On the Measurement of the Earth*, which was probably
separate from his *Geographika*, Eratosthenes explained his methods and
conclusions. He assumed that Alexandria and Syene (modern Aswan, in
Egypt) were situated on the same longitude (the term is used throughout
this chapter interchangeably with 'meridian'); that they were 5,000 *stadia*

[8] Keyser (2001), 361–365.   [9] *Sand Reckoner*, 1.
[10] Berger (1880); Geus (2002), esp. 260–288; (2004); Nicastro (2008); Roller (2010).
[11] Bowen and Todd (2004).

distant from one other; that on the summer solstice (21 June) the sun was at its zenith in Syene at noon; and that according to the shadow cast by a *gnômôn* (sun-dial) placed in Alexandria on the same day, the angle of the sun in relation to the surface of the earth was 7°12′ (about 1/50 of a 360° circle). Taking these details into account, Eratosthenes estimated the circumference of the earth at 250,000 *stadia* (5,000 x 50). Depending on the length of his *stadion*, the result could be taken to represent about 40,000 kilometres, which is very near to the actual perimeter (40,075.16 kilometres at the equator, 40,008 kilometres by longitudes).[12]

Two hundred years later, Posidonius of Apamea applied a similar method. He assumed that Rhodes and Alexandria were situated on the same longitude; that they were 5,000 *stadia* apart; and that the star Canopus touched the horizon in Rhodes at a longitudinal altitude of 7°30′ (about 1/48 of a 360° circle). He thus concluded that the circumference of the earth was 240,000 *stadia* (5,000 x 48), although he later reduced the number to 180,000 *stadia*, probably by recalculating the distance between Alexandria and Rhodes. This latter, smaller figure was accepted in antiquity (for instance by Ptolemy) and later, and may be the reason why Christopher Columbus mistook America for India, on the assumption that the globe was too small to include an unknown continent.

Another issue that continuously occupied the attention of mathematical geographers was the shape and size of the earth's dry land, that is, the *oikoumenê*. Before we take up these details, some attention to the ancient ideas of the situation of the *oikoumenê* on the globe (once the spherical shape theory was accepted[13]) and the general scheme of its layout is necessary. The *oikoumenê* was usually conceived of as a symmetrical shape – generally round or oblong – with neat edges. The Homeric and Archaic concept put the Ocean at its borders; Herodotus imagined deserts there instead.[14] The idea of a surrounding Ocean persisted throughout antiquity, but the picture grew more elaborate, as for example in Pomponius Mela:

It [the inhabited world] is entirely surrounded by the Ocean, and from the Ocean it allows four seas to enter: one from the north [the Caspian], two from the south [the Persian and Arabian Gulfs], and a fourth from the west [the Mediterranean]. (1.5)

---

[12] Engels (1985). Some sources give Eratosthenes' figure as 252,000 *stadia*, which arithmetically suited the conventional division of a circle into 60 parts: Evans (1998), 65; Nicastro (2008).

[13] In the flat-disk or concave-circle theory, the dry (is)land was situated at the centre, equidistant from the rims.

[14] Romm (1992), 33–40.

There were also notions of fixed and symmetrical frameworks on land.[15] The various schemes of the limits of the *oikoumenê* thus included some constant elements in a mix of reality and fantasy: (1) deserts; (2) mountains (the Caucasus in the east; the Pyrenees in the west; the Rhipaean mountains in the north; the Ethiopian highlands in the south); (3) nations (the Indians in the east; the Celts in the west; the Scythians in the north; the Ethiopians in the south); and (4) islands (Thule in the north; Cerne and the Canary Islands in the west; Taprobane [Sri Lanka] in the southeast).[16]

Symmetry as an aesthetic criterion for the mental arrangement of the world is also apparent in ideas put forward for example by Herodotus and Polybius. Herodotus (4.50) imagines the world's two great northern and southern rivers – the Ister (Danube) and the Nile, respectively – as located symmetrically, in a way that implies a logical natural order. This picture both suited aesthetic ideals and made the reader's conceptual understanding easier. Adding climatological considerations related to north versus south (discussed below), Herodotus also assumed that, if there really were Hyperboreans ('those beyond the north'), there must be Hypernotians ('those beyond the south') as well (4.36).[17] Similarly, Polybius (16.29.5) hinted at the symmetrical position and parallel role of the straits at the Pillars of Heracles leading to the Atlantic, and of those at the eastern end of the Mediterranean leading to the Black Sea.

The Pillars of Heracles, marking the continental tips on either side of what are today known as the Straits of Gibraltar, were an important geographical point, marking the western edge of the Mediterranean and forming its only outlet to the frightening and mysterious Ocean. The Pillars represented a monitory boundary and a gate between an inner/safer/known world and outer/dangerous/unknown waters.[18] They therefore featured in every attempt to sail around Africa or northern Europe. One line of tradition suggested that Heracles cut an opening in the shores of the previously closed Mediterranean.[19] An almost precisely opposite version claimed that he narrowed an existing opening to keep monsters and other dangers out.[20] Similarly, it was said that Dionysus in his wanderings erected pillars at the edge of the earth in India.[21]

---

[15] Heidel (1976); Romm (1992).
[16] Mountains: Arist. *Mete.* 1.13, 350a28–b14. Nations: Ephorus *FGrHist* 70 F 30.
[17] Hartog (1988), 12–19; Romm (1989a).
[18] Romm (1992), 15–17.
[19] Plin. *HN* 3.4; Sen. *Herc.* 235–238; Sen. *Herc.Oetaeus* 1240.
[20] Diod. Sic. 4.18.5; Strabo 3.5.2–6; Mela 1.27.
[21] Apollod. 2.29; Strabo 3.5.6.

In addition to fixed symmetrical or balanced edges, the inhabited world was thought to have a centre. According to a well-known myth, Zeus simultaneously sent two eagles from the eastern and western edges of the world, and they met at Delphi.[22] This was where the navel (*omphalos*) of the world was fixed,[23] and the place became central not only for religious reasons but for its geometrical position equidistant from the ends of the known world. A similar idea is apparent in Roman traditions of the *umbilicus urbis Romae* ('navel of the city of Rome'); symbolically, the centre of the world had moved to Rome.[24]

The size and shape of the *oikoumenê* naturally changed with time, as knowledge of previously unknown regions increased and boundaries expanded. Both parameters depended on the definition of borders, which in antiquity meant the ability to sail around the inhabited landmass:

It is the sea more than anything else that defines the contours of the land and gives it its shape by forming gulfs, deep seas, straits and likewise isthmuses, peninsulas and promontories; but both the rivers and the mountains assist the seas herein. (Strabo 2.5.17)

The mix of fact and imagination, sometimes based on considerations of symmetry or other theoretical ideas, produced a number of suggestions as to the general shape of the *oikoumenê*:

The ancients drew the *oikoumenê* round, and regarded Greece as the centre and Delphi in its middle, containing the navel of the earth. It was first Democritus, a very experienced man, who saw that the earth was oblong, having a length one-and-a-half times greater than its width. (Agathemerus, *Sketch of Geography*, 2)[25]

Strabo presented a more refined and picturesque image of the shape of the *oikoumenê*, describing it as resembling a cloak or mantle (*chlamys*):

The shape of the inhabited world is somewhat like a *chlamys* … Accordingly, we must conceive of a parallelogram, in which the *chlamys*-shaped figure is inscribed in such a way that the greatest length of the *chlamys* coincides with, and is equal to, the greatest length of the parallelogram, and likewise its greatest breadth and the breadth of the parallelogram. (Strabo 2.5.14)

Authors who accepted the oblong shape of the inhabited world none the less disagreed about its size. Their measurements were expressed in three ways: by indicating the ratio between length and width; by quoting

---

[22] Strabo 9.3.6; Paus. 10.16.3.
[23] Compare similar beliefs regarding the rock on the Temple Mount in Jerusalem and the Ka'aba in Mecca.
[24] Brodersen (1996/97).   [25] Diller (1975), 60.

dimensions in *stadia*; or by indicating size through spherical degrees. Aristotle offered the following scheme incorporating size, shape and situation on the globe:

> The distance from the Pillars of Heracles to India exceeds that from Aethiopia to Maeotis [Sea of Azov] and the farthest parts of Scythia by a ratio greater than five to three … beyond India and the Pillars of Heracles it is the Ocean which severs the habitable land. (Arist. *Mete.* 2.5, 362b21–30)

Dicaearchus suggested a ratio of 3:2, while according to Eratosthenes the length of the *oikoumenê* was 77,800 *stadia* (14,393 kilometres), a third of the whole circle by his calculations (Strabo 1.4.5). Posidonius proposed a length of 70,000 *stadia* (12,950 kilometres), half of the entire circle on his figures (Strabo 2.3.6). Finally, Ptolemy determined that the length of the known world was 180° east–west or 12 hours, while its breadth was 90° north–south (*Alm.* 2.1), an exact quarter of the entire sphere.[26]

Ptolemy (Claudius Ptolemaeus) (*c.* 90–168 CE) was a Greek scholar based in Roman Egypt who researched various topics in mathematics, astronomy and geography.[27] He relied on centuries of geographical discussion, both descriptive and scientific, and produced two major works of geographical significance: the *Almagest* and the *Geography*. The former was basically an astronomical treatise dealing with the motion of planets, stars and other astronomical bodies. Ptolemy's main goal in his *Geography* was to offer a series of tables with accurate lists of numerical coordinates of sites, as a basis for a graphic map (3.3 and chapter 4). He did not offer new insights or scientific breakthroughs, and he relied specifically on the (now lost) works of Marinus of Tyre. But he preserved information that would otherwise be lost to us, and combined it into a coherent whole that influenced science and geography until the Renaissance.

The common assumption was that the inhabited world was situated mostly on the northern hemisphere of the globe, with its northern parts touching the cold North Pole and its southern edges located around the hot regions of the equator. Ptolemy offered a more precise positioning. He showed that the globe was divided into four equal quarters by the equator and by a meridian passing through both poles, and that the *oikoumenê* was located in the quarter limited to the south by the equator, to the north by the North Pole, and to the east and west by the meridian circle. He then specified the extreme points on all four ends: Thule to the north, Aigisumba (south of the Sahara) and Cape Prason (on the east coast of

---

[26] Riley (1995), esp. 230–236.
[27] Aujac (1993), 49–64; Riley (1995); Berggren and Jones (2000).

Africa) to the south, the Isles of the Blessed (Canary Islands) to the west, and China to the east (*Geog.* 1.8).

Accepting the spherical shape of the world and the assumed size of the *oikoumenê* upon it, some theorists wondered whether there were other *oikoumenai* or even uninhabited dry lands on the globe. The Ocean excited curiosity among the ancients, because it was immeasurable and thus unlimited. This lack of solid knowledge produced the Platonic myth of Atlantis, as presented in the *Timaeus* and the *Critias*. According to this story, Atlantis was a powerful kingdom, 'larger than Libya and Asia together', which waged war against Mediterranean people but sank into the sea and was lost forever. The supposed size of Atlantis hints at Plato's sense of the enormous size of the Ocean. Scholars today debate whether Plato's legend recalls a real early sunken continent or represents a fictive utopia created in support of philosophic and ethical imaginings. But in any case, Atlantis inflamed the imagination of generations who continued to look for the lost landmass, whether in the form of a solid continent (America) or a sunken one (sought by modern underwater expeditions).

In a different context, Plato's Socrates expresses an awareness of horizons wider than those that are visible:

I believe that the earth is very large, and that we who dwell between the Pillars of Heracles and the river Phasis [modern Rioni, in Georgia] live in a small part of it about the sea, like ants or frogs about a pond, and that many other people live in many other such regions. (*Phaedo* 109b)

Plato's motivation for inventing Atlantis was perhaps purely ethical, but Aristotle relied on the aesthetic criterion of symmetry in his conjecture that another parallel inhabited world could be found in the southern hemisphere: 'There are two habitable sectors of the earth's surface, one in which we live towards the upper pole, the other towards the other, that is the south pole. These are the only habitable regions' (*Mete.* 2.5, 362a32–b6).

Again, taking his departure from theoretical hypotheses, which were by no means based on actual experience, and aiming at interpreting the Homeric epics, Crates of Mallus offered in *c.* 150 BCE a symmetrical scheme of a globe containing four *oikoumenai* separated by two intersecting belts of Ocean (figure 1). These were: (1) the known *oikoumenê*, including its three continents; (2) the land of the *Antoikoi* ('those who live opposite'), parallel to the *oikoumenê* in the southern hemisphere; (3) the land of the *Perioikoi* ('those who live around'), parallel to the *oikoumenê*

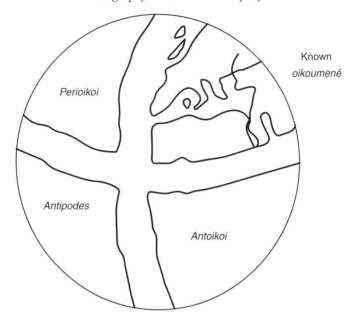

Figure 1: The position of the four *oikoumenai* on the
globe according to Crates of Mallus.

on the western part of the globe; (4) the land of the *Antipodes* ('opposite
feet'), parallel to the *Perioikoi* in the southern hemisphere.[28]

Pliny the Elder promoted this idea and suggested that the entire
sphere was inhabited, including the *Antipodes*, although this raised a new
problem:

Human beings are distributed all round the earth and stand with their feet
pointing toward each other, and the top of the sky is alike for them all and the
earth trodden under foot at the centre in the same way from any direction, while
ordinary people enquire why the persons on the opposite side do not fall off –
just as if it were not reasonable that the people on the other side wonder that we
do not fall off. (Plin. *HN* 2.161)

Such ideas remained purely academic, and were produced by intellectuals
exploring scientific premises and conclusions. At the same time, however,
they inflamed the popular imagination. The younger Seneca, in his tragedy *Medea*, articulated a notion that was fantastic at the time but seems
almost prophetic today:

[28] Dilke (1985), 36–37.

All bounds have been removed, cities
have set their walls in new lands,
and the world, now passable throughout,
has left nothing where it once had sat:
the Indian drinks of the cold Araxes,
the Persians quaff the Elbe and the Rhine.
There will come an age in the far-off years
when Ocean shall unloose the bonds of things,
when the whole broad earth shall be revealed,
when Tethys shall disclose new worlds
and Thule shall not be the limit of the lands.
(*Med.* 369–379)

Narrowing our focus, we now consider the geographical divisions within the *oikoumenê*. The Greeks recognized three continents within the inhabited world: Europe and Asia first, and then Libya (that is, Africa).[29] Hypotheses about other continents beyond the Ocean – for example, Plato's lost Atlantis – were mere fantasies. How did the concept of a continent develop?[30] The basic distinction that emerges from the earliest Greek sources is between land and sea (e.g., *Il.* 1.485; *Od.* 3.90). This distinction was then refined to include a differentiation between mainland and islands, reflecting a mental opposition between territorial connectivity and isolation.[31] Giving specific names to larger land masses eventually yielded the three individual continents as the ancients knew them. There was thus nothing essentially unique about a continent in comparison to any other topographical unit, and in particular to large islands such as Sicily, Crete and Euboea. As islands had names, so too did continents, which were defined geographically by topographic features marking their limits, even if there were occasional arguments about the exact location of these limits. A continent's precise borders were not always agreed, particularly as some authors were aware of earlier geological situations. For example, C. Acilius (*fl.* 155 BCE), a Roman historian writing in Greek, explained that Sicily was part of the mainland in prehistoric times, but that a flood had made it separate.[32] Even when the division was permanent, there were different methods for defining borders between

---

[29] The names of the continents, like many ancient toponyms (e.g., Atlantic, Aegean, Peloponnese and numerous cities and towns), derived from the names of mythological characters. See Philipp (1936). On the divisions, see Romm (2010).
[30] Constantakopoulou (2007), 10–19.
[31] For this idea see Horden and Purcell (2000).
[32] *FGrHist* 813 F 13 and Mela 2.115.

continents. The most straightforward relied on topographic features that formed natural borders, particularly rivers:

Asia lies between the Nile and the Tanais [Don], and falls under that portion of the heaven lying between the north-east and the south. Africa lies between the Nile and the Pillars of Heracles, and falls under the southern portion of the heaven, which extends to the south-west and west … Europe lies opposite them on the north shore of this sea, extending continuously from east to west, its most compact and deepest portion lying due north, between the Tanais and the Narbo, the latter river being not far west of Massalia and the mouths by which the Rhône discharges into the Sardinian Sea … The remaining part of Europe beyond the Pyrenees, reaching to its western end and to the Pillars of Heracles, is bounded on one side by the Mediterranean, and on the other by the Outer Sea. (Polyb. 3.37.2–10)

The term 'Mediterranean' as a substantive noun applied to the known sea (rather than used as an adjective meaning 'between lands') is first attested relatively late, in the third-century CE work of Solinus (23.14). Prior to this, the Greeks used several terms for this body of water, such as 'the inner sea' as opposed to the outer sea (i.e., the Ocean). The Romans used the term *mare nostrum* ('our sea'), or the plural 'our seas' to include various gulfs and extensions,[33] reflecting a new political reality.

Hecataeus of Miletus divided his *periodos gês* into two books, each devoted to one continent, Europe and Asia, and appended his description of Egypt to the book on Asia. In his time (late sixth century BCE), there was accordingly still no defined identity for the third continent. But in the fifth century the three continents were generally recognized, and it became common for geographical compositions in both prose and poetry to devote separate literary units to each continent.

As late as the first century BCE, M. Terentius Varro preserved a continental division of the inhabited world into Europe and Asia, although he based this division on astronomical calculations, ignoring the irregular boundaries of land and water: 'the earth is divided into Asia and Europe. For Asia lies toward the noonday sun and the South Wind, Europe toward the Great Bear and the North Wind' (*Ling.* 5.3.1). Sallust, meanwhile, maintaining his thematic focus, defined the borders of Africa as follows:

In their division of the earth's surface, geographers commonly regard Africa as a third part, but a few recognize only Asia and Europe, including Africa in the latter. Africa is bounded on the west by the strait between our sea and the Ocean, on the east by a broad sloping tract that the natives call Catabathmos. (*Iug.* 17.3–4)

---

[33] E.g., Mela 1.6; 1.13. And see Horden and Purcell (2000); Abulafia (2011).

A consensus about the external contour of the *oikoumenê* took time to develop. This is apparent in the changing geographical definition of the Caspian Sea which, after being conceived as closed by Aristotle (*Mete.* 2.1, 354a3–4), was thought in the time of Alexander the Great to be a gulf of the Ocean. Indeed, Alexander's men claimed that the Caspian was also connected with the Indian Ocean (Arr. *Anab.* 5.26). Another hint of earlier phases of defining the contours of the inhabited world is apparent in Eratosthenes' comment that a certain Damastes thought the Arabian Gulf (i.e., the Red Sea) was a lake (Strabo 1.3.1). As for the extent of the landmass, Ptolemy believed that Asia included an unknown region on its eastern border, and that China stretched further, to a southern (*australis* in Latin) country.

The definition of the borders of continents was one issue; the definition of their size and shape was another. This was also a controversial matter, and Herodotus did not hesitate to express his doubts about some *periodoi gês*:

I laugh when I see how many have before now written *periodoi gês*, not one of them giving a reasonable account; for they describe the world as round as if fashioned by compasses, and encircled by the Ocean, and Asia and Europe as of a like size … I wonder, then, at those who have defined and divided the world into Libya, Asia and Europe; for the difference between them is great, seeing that in length Europe stretches along both the others together, and appears to me to be beyond all comparison broader. For Libya shows clearly that it is encompassed by the sea, save only where it borders on Asia. (Hdt. 4.36; 4.42)

Even later, certain parts of the world, and (unsurprisingly) remote parts in particular, remained amorphous. This led to occasionally ridiculous conclusions:

Ctesias of Cnidus affirms that the land of India is equal in size to the rest of Asia, which is absurd; and Onesicritus is absurd, who says that India is a third of the entire world. (Arr. *Ind.* 3.6)

Calculating heights, particularly of individual mountains, was more complicated than estimating the size of flat territories. When myth was still involved in geography, some mountains were deemed high beyond reach and therefore impossible to measure. There were thus mountains so high that their summit was invisible, for instance Mount Olympus and the Atlas range (Hdt. 4.184). But a desire for accuracy encouraged attempts at calculation and produced some useful results.[34] The older method used a *gnômôn*, measuring its shadow at sunset east of the

---

[34] Cajori (1929); Lewis (2001), 157–166.

mountain, or at sunrise west of it. The *gnômôn* and its shadow created a right-angled triangle. This was compared with the triangle created by the shadow cast by the mountain, and by applying geometric axioms regarding similar triangles, the missing side – that is, the mountain's height – could be calculated.[35] In about 305 BCE Dicaearchus of Messana offered a more accurate method, by applying the equal-angle reflection of light. Finally, Eratosthenes improved Dicaearchus' method by using the dioptra (a sighting tube).[36]

Here too, theory, and especially considerations of symmetry, influenced the understanding of heights. Posidonius, for example, argued that the highest mountain on earth should be as high as the deepest place is deep. Since it was assumed that the maximum depth of the sea was 15 *stadia* (2,880 meters), the tallest mountain must be 15 *stadia* high.[37]

Regardless of the method used, all ancient measurements of mountains were mere approximations and estimates, and such measurements became precise only very recently, thanks to the use of satellite technology. Numbers were rounded, measurements were not taken from sea level, and calculations changed according to the exact point from which a mountain was measured, the peak targeted, and the size of the *stadion* used. It is accordingly difficult to assess the accuracy of ancient measurements of height, or to compare various measurements of the same mountain. Mountain heights also figured in discussions of the spherical shape of the earth: was it less spherical because of the protrusion of the highest mountains? Attempts to measure them showed that their height was negligible in relation to the overall size of the globe:

In comparison with the great size of the earth, the protrusion of mountains is insufficient to deprive it of its spherical shape or to invalidate measurements based on its spherical shape. For Eratosthenes shows that the perpendicular distance from the highest mountain tops to the lowest regions is 10 *stadia*. (Simplicius, *Commentary on Aristotle's Cael.* pp. 549.32–550.4)

Sea depth was measured by estimates based on dropping heavy objects tied to ropes, and Pliny reports:

According to the account of Fabianus, the deepest sea has a depth of nearly two miles. Others report an immense depth of water … off the coast of the Coraxi

---

[35] Thales applied this method to calculate the height of the Egyptian pyramids: Plin. *HN* 36.82; Diog. Laert. 1.27.

[36] Fortenbaugh and Schütrumpf (2001); Keyser (2001); Lewis (2001), 267–270.

[37] F 288 Theiler.

tribe on the Black Sea, about 37 miles from land, where soundings have never reached bottom. (Plin. *HN* 2.224)

An important feature of ancient geography was the illustration of specific units through the description and definition of their shapes. For this purpose, authors used forms they assumed their readers knew, and compared the topographic or spatial detail in question with these shapes. This habit resulted in a series of geographical metaphors.[38] Description of shapes relied on a mental idea of the figure, and the sole tool of the surveyor was 'verbal cartography'. Shapes of topographic and geographical entities were thus likened to other similar shapes. These included, first of all, geometric figures: Sicily seen as a triangle (Polyb. 1.42.3), India as a rhombus (Strabo 2.1.22), and Narbonensis as a parallelogram (Strabo 4.1.3). Various non-geometric shapes were also used in descriptions: bodily organs, animals, plants, garments, furniture and weapons:

The circumference of the whole sea [Black Sea] is approximately 25,000 *stadia*. Some compare the shape of this circumference to that of a bent Scythian bow, likening the bow string to the regions on what is called the right hand side of the Pontus … and the rest they liken to the horn of the bow with its double curve, the upper curve being rounded off, while the lower curve is straighter. (Strabo 2.5.22)

Some modern analyses of ancient Greek and Roman spatial, and not linear, frameworks of the various parts of the universe, the globe, the *oikoumenê* and the continents, apply modern ideas of spatial concepts.[39] Attempts are being made at reconstructing certain spatial models from the available sources which may have influenced geographical world-views in antiquity. The assumption is that certain cultural paradigms create spatial concepts which in turn determine the way a person observes, grasps and describes his environment. This is not to say that the Greeks or Romans had a pre-planned and well-conceived model of the world and its components, but that by looking at various phases of geographical representations in antiquity, it is possible to follow certain paradigms by which space is described (for instance the round and symmetrical 'island' of the *oikoumenê* surrounded by the Ocean). As we have seen, descriptive and scientific geography combined to offer a coherent verbal picture of sites often remote from the environment of their audience. Mathematics,

[38] Clarke (1999); Dueck (2005b).
[39] Janni (1984); Romm (1992); Horden and Purcell (2000); Brodersen (2003); Cosgrove (2008); Purves (2010).

and in particular astronomy, further supported ancient geographical aspirations by offering methods to define locations on the globe (3.3).

The Greeks and the Romans were interested in the world, provided it was inhabited. Deserted regions were considered neither in written records in the various geographical genres, including the scientific, nor in proposed expeditions. This had political ramifications, since annexed lands were in most cases inhabited. Authors then constantly discussed these foreigners, expressing feelings ranging from admiration to disgust, and describing various components of the daily life of the peoples in question. In the modern division of academic disciplines, these themes would fall under human geography or anthropology. In antiquity, however, they were an integral part of geographical description in all its formats and genres.

The main link to geography was the early conviction that local conditions and the environment influenced human character. Accordingly, extreme weather (hot or cold) was deemed to produce particular ferocity and affect the skin colour, type of hair and height of the inhabitants of the region. In this way, there was a conceptual deterministic correlation between the situation of certain groups of people on the globe and their political, economic and even ethical behaviour.[40] This idea was given shape in the theory of climatic zones.[41]

Beginning in the early fifth century BCE, the Greeks were aware not only of seasonal climatic differences, but of regional differences as well. A conceptual correlation between climate and other local varia, such as fauna, flora, and even human appearance and behaviour, was formed. This connection was converted into a fixed scheme through attempts to connect the situation of certain regions on the globe with local human and natural traits. As time passed, the ability to calculate exact location using latitudes contributed to a more systematic picture.

Herodotus described the extreme cold in the northern region inhabited by the Scythians: 'All this aforementioned country is exceedingly cold; for eight months of every year, there is unbearable frost … the sea freezes, and the entire Cimmerian Bosporus' (4.28). Even harsher conditions were thought to exist further north:

---

[40] See, for example, an early Greek and a late Roman example: Hippocrates, *Airs, Waters, Places*, 12–14; Vegetius, *De re militari*, 1.2.

[41] Sanderson (1999); Romm (2010).

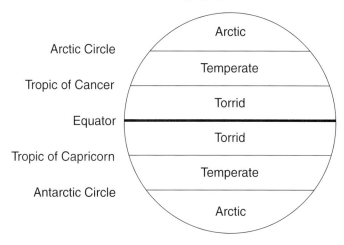

Figure 2: The five climatic zones.

Above and northward of the neighbours of their country none, they say, can see or travel further, by reason of showers of feathers; for earth and sky are overspread by these, and it is this which hinders sight … whoever has seen snow falling thickly near him knows what I mean; for the snow is like feathers; and by reason of the winter, which is such as I have said, the parts to the north of this continent are uninhabited. (Hdt. 4.7, 4.31)

A similar association of extreme weather (in this case heat) with limited or no human habitation was made in connection with the eastern parts of the *oikoumenê* (Hdt. 3.104). Extreme weather conditions were thus understood to have rendered entire regions uninhabited and impassable, which meant that – to a fifth-century scholarly understanding – there was a three-way connection between location on earth, climate and habitation. Parmenides of Elea combined the location–climate–habitation complex with the concept of a spherical earth, adding scientific parameters to the theme. He specified five latitudinal climate zones on the globe. These were determined by the changing angle between the sun and the earth, and stretched across the globe parallel to the equator. The five regions were: a torrid zone, encircling the equator and characterized by extremely hot weather; two polar or arctic zones, situated by the poles of the globe and characterized by extremely cold weather; and two zones located between the polar and the torrid zones on the two hemispheres, and characterized by a temperate climate (figure 2). Parmenides claimed that the torrid zone was uninhabited because of the direct radiation of the sun, which did not allow humans to survive there. Two and a half centuries later, Strabo added that Posidonius gave ethnic identifications to these zones, calling the torrid zone the Ethiopic zone, the arctic zone the Scythico-Celtic zone, and the temperate zone the intermediate zone (Strabo 2.3.1).

Although the basic idea of latitudinal zones related to climate had been accepted since Parmenides, there was no agreement about the number of such zones. This was in fact a largely semantic difference. Polybius, for example, argued for six zones, while Eratosthenes, Posidonius and Strabo retained the idea of five:

Polybius counts six zones: two that fall beneath the arctic circles, two between the arctic circle and the tropics, and two between the tropics and the Equator. But the division into five zones seems to me to be in harmony with physics as well as geography: with physics in relation both to the celestial phenomena and to the temperature of the atmosphere; in relation to the celestial phenomena because … the appearance of the constellations to our sight is defined simultaneously. (Strabo 2.3.1)

The Greek word *klima* means 'inclination, slope', and was used specifically for the supposed slope of the earth toward the poles. Regional differences in weather were thus literally associated with the concept of climatic zones. Because of the theoretical range of error in measuring latitudes, the *klimata* were not mathematical lines but broad strips of land extending east and west across the *oikoumenê*. This enabled Aristotle in his *Meteorologica* to offer the following insight regarding climate, habitation and the arrangement of the world:

We know the whole breadth of the habitable world up to the inhabitable regions which bound it, where habitation ceases on the one side because of cold, on the other because of heat. While beyond India and the Pillars of Heracles it is the Ocean that severs the habitable land and prevents it forming a continuous belt around the globe. (*Mete.* 2.5, 362b26–30)

Parmenides' theoretical sketch offered a complete scheme of the globe (and not just the *oikoumenê* on it) in a symmetrical arrangement. This was the conceptual background for assuming the existence of another *oikoumenê* in the parallel temperate zone in the southern hemisphere (3.1):

Heat makes the middle zone uninhabitable, and cold does so to the outermost ones. The remaining two habitable zones have the same annual seasons but not at the same time. The Antichthones inhabit one, we the other. The chorography of the former zone is unknown because of the heat of the intervening expanse, and the chorography of the latter is now to be described. (Mela 1.4)

Climate and position on the globe also implied a connection between weather conditions and the forms of plants, animals and human beings:

Variety in animal life may be produced by variety of locality: thus in one place an animal will not be found at all, in another it will be small, or short-lived, or will not thrive ... In many places, the climate will account for peculiarities; thus in Illyria, Thrace, and Epirus the ass is small, while in Gaul and in Scythia the ass is not found at all, owing to the coldness of the climate of these countries. (Arist. *Hist. An.* 8.28)

In a fifth-century BCE work ascribed to the medical school of Hippocrates, the claim is advanced that human beings' health is affected by their place of habitation:

Whoever wishes to pursue properly the science of medicine must proceed thus: first he ought to consider what effects each season of the year can produce ... therefore, on arrival at a town with which he is unfamiliar, a physician should examine its position with respect to the winds and the risings of the sun. (*On Airs, Waters, Places* 1.1)

These notions implied that the physical nature of human beings varied from place to place. Strabo thus quotes Posidonius' explanation of the uniform, typical human and animal physiognomy in warmer zones:

These two zones have a certain peculiarity, in that they are parched in the literal sense of the word, are sandy, and produce nothing except silphium and some pungent fruits ... those regions have in their neighbourhood no mountains against which the clouds may break and produce rain, nor are they coursed by rivers; and for this reason, they produce creatures with woolly hair, crumpled horns, protruding lips, and flat noses, for their extremities are contorted by the heat. (2.2.3)

Accordingly, some Greeks from the fifth century BCE on believed in a close relationship between appearance, behaviour, health and local natural conditions. The Aristotelian approach expanded the influence of climate to other human qualities:

The nations inhabiting the cold places and those of Europe are full of spirit but somewhat deficient in intelligence and skill, so that they continue comparatively free, but lacking in political organization and capacity to rule their neighbours. The peoples of Asia, on the other hand, are intelligent and skilful in temperament, but lack spirit, so that they are in continuous subjection and slavery. But the Greek people participates in both characters, just as it occupies the middle position geographically, for it is both spirited and intelligent. Hence it continues to be free and to have very good political institutions, and to be capable of ruling all mankind if it were to attain constitutional unity. (Aristotle, *Pol.* 7.6, 1327b24–36)

A deterministic notion that claimed that the environment shaped human beings and their qualities thus seems to have been prevalent. This led to ethnic stereotypes based on climate and geography, and to what may seem a racist approach.[42] Qualification of such views was expressed, but these too involved elements of ethnographic definition.

Already in the fifth century BCE, the notion of a dichotomy between Greeks and non-Greeks existed.[43] The latter were referred to as *barbaroi*, though not necessarily in a derogatory sense; some non-Greek nations were even admired for their wisdom and power, for example the Persians and the Egyptians.[44] The origin of the term *barbaroi* was, according to some ancient authors, onomatopoeic, reflecting the distorted pronunciation of Greek by non-native speakers. With time, however, other notions were added to this ethnic nickname, including ferocity, simplicity and poverty. The physical appearance of foreigners was the first thing Greek and Roman visitors noticed, and it incited a variety of emotions, including fear, awe and ridicule. Such traits were sometimes exaggerated and were often included in collections of *thaumata* or *mirabilia*. The concept and terminology of barbarism, as opposed to culture, are thus a key to understanding classical ethno-geography.

This original notion of the ethnic division of the world into two fundamental parts was gradually modified, as an awareness of changing degrees of 'barbarian' traits became widespread. Thus, a sort of mental scale emerged, on which each human group could theoretically be placed. This explains ideas such as 'half-barbarians' (Demetrius of Scepsis in Strabo 13.1.5) and 'mixed' tribes (Ephorus in Strabo 14.5.23). The scale itself included several components, mainly the nature of the region inhabited (whether coast or plain, or fertile as opposed to rocky, rough, remote and barren terrain); the people's way of life (whether they practise agriculture and commerce, or continuous war and piracy); and their social habits (philanthropy, law and order as against lawlessness, aggression and cruelty).[45]

The Romans were more open-minded towards strangers than the Greeks.[46] This was probably the result of the expansion of their Empire, which encompassed regions that were diverse both in topography and in climate and in human resources. It was not uncommon to see black

---

[42] Isaac (2004).
[43] Cunliffe (1988); Hall (1989); Coleman (1997); Cartledge (1993); (2001); Malkin (2001); Harrison (2002).
[44] Attitude towards specific nations: Isaac (2004), 253–491.
[45] Thollard (1987).   [46] Burns (2003); Isaac (2004).

people or individuals wearing striking ethnic dress in Rome, and some of these were in fact Roman citizens. Nonetheless, the basic differentiation between barbarians and non-barbarians persisted throughout antiquity.

This approach is somewhat balanced by the words of Strabo, who lived in a multicultural world controlled by the Roman Empire. After criticizing Posidonius' emphasis on climatic factors (2.3.7), Strabo argued that traits that depend on environmental conditions can be changed:

The Romans took over many nations that were naturally savage owing to the regions they inhabited, because those regions were either rocky, or without harbours, or cold, or for some other reason ill-suited to habitation by many, and thus not only brought into communication with each other peoples who had been isolated, but taught the more savage how to live under forms of regulated government. (2.5.26)

According to this thesis, nations can become civilized despite their location and regardless of the weather in their country. Climate and topography were thus a necessary and important part of descriptions of environments and new regions, but they did not inevitably fix national character in an irreversible fashion.

Climate differences and their association with location on the globe were also thought to influence various practical decisions, so that Vitruvius (*De arch.* 6.1.1–12) claims that the types of buildings in an area depended on the climate there, and thus on latitude (*inclinatio mundi*), while Vegetius (1.2) connects types of soldiers and their physique. In such discussions, distinctions were usually drawn between north and south, implying a latitudinal division.

Using a somewhat eclectic approach, and adhering to earlier geographical tradition, Strabo combined several concepts regarding the construction of the world and associated four elements in it: the limit of human habitation, the limit of the known world, the limit of the temperate zone, and the southernmost latitude.

Since the cinnamon-producing country [south Ethiopia] is the most remote inhabited country toward the south, as we know ... the parallel that runs through it is the beginning of the temperate zone and of the *oikoumenê*. (2.1.13)

This implies a full identification between these parameters and their location: habitation ceased where the temperate zone ended. For scholars interested only in the *oikoumenê*, this point also marked the edge of the world, and the same location was identical with the southernmost latitude of the *oikoumenê*. In this system, the middle point of the inhabited world was also regarded as the middle in relation to all other conceptual frameworks, but political considerations moved the centre: originally it was Greece, but later Italy took its place.

> In Italy the inhabitants are exactly tempered in either direction, both in the structure of the body and by their strength of mind in the matter of endurance and courage … Italy presents good qualities which are tempered by admixture from either side both north and south, and are consequently unsurpassed. And so, by its policy, it curbs the courage of the northern barbarians; by its strength, the imaginative south. Thus the divine mind has allotted to the Roman state an excellent, temperate region in order to rule the world. (Vitr. *De arch.* 6.1.11)

3.3 LOCATING COORDINATES

In the early stages of Greek civilization, travel, whether by sea or land, sometimes yielded written documentation of the location of sites for the benefit of future travellers, such as merchants, armies and tourists. Several parameters were used in these records to define location.[47] A basic one was the order of sites along a (preferably linear) route, such as a coast, river, mountain range or road. This way of reckoning required an initial point, to which all further sites were related. This method was a constant in Greek and Latin writings, early and late. In *periploi*, a common formula was to indicate that, for example, 'Next comes the city Huops, and next the river Lesurus';[48] so too in *itineraria*, which by definition listed sites according to their order on specific routes (2.3). The same method was employed in more elaborate descriptions, many of which used *periploi* as sources, for example in the work of Pomponius Mela: 'If you follow the coast, close after Cervaria there is the cliff that pushes the Pyrenees into the sea, and then the Ticis River near Rhoda, Clodianum near Emporiae, and then Mount Jupiter' (2.89).

Another basic means of conveying location was distance expressed in units of time, usually the number of travel days by sea or land (3.1). This was a variable, subjective parameter, of course, dependent on the means of travel, speed and weather conditions. In some cases, the direction of the journey was indicated, adding another guideline. Initial orientation was provided by referring to a direction relative to some geographical or topographic feature, such as a mountain or an island, for example in Sophocles: 'After this, toward your right hand you will find the whole land of Oinotria, the Tyrrhenian Gulf and the land Ligustike' (F 598

---

[47] Compasses were a later invention: Aczel (2001).
[48] Hecataeus of Miletus, *FGrHist* 1 F 48.

Radt), and in Strabo: 'As one sails from the city [Rhodes] with the island on the right, one comes first to Lindus' (14.2.11). Astronomical features, generally the sun, also helped establish the direction of movement, since journeys by both land and sea were usually made by day; Hanno's records mention that 'from here we sailed toward the midday sun for twelve days, coasting along the shore' (11).

Gradually, fixed directions were established, and by the fifth century BCE several terms were used to indicate orientation.[49] One set of terms related to the motion of the sun, and referred to the east as *anatolê* ('the rising', *oriens* in Latin), the west as *dusis* ('the setting', *occidens* in Latin), and the sun's position at midday (*mesêmbria*) as south.[50] Four cardinal points were thus established:

Where the sun rises is designated formally as east or sunrise; where it sinks, as west or sunset; where it begins its descent, south; in the opposite direction, north. (Mela 1.3)

Similarly, the words for 'morning' (*eôs*) and 'evening' (*hespera*) became synonymous with east and west, respectively.[51] The Homeric set of winds associated with specific locations also served as metaphors for directions. Thus, *Boreas* (*Aquilo* in Latin) was north; *Notos* (*Auster* in Latin) was south; *Apêliotês* or *Eurus* was east, and *Zephyrus* (*Favonius* in Latin) was west. Vitruvius described the Tower of Winds built by the Greek astronomer Andronicus of Cyrrhus (*c.* 100 BCE), which included a dial of eight winds, each indicating a particular direction (*De arch.* 1.6.4–13). Latin texts also used the seven stars of the Great Bear (*Septentriones*) as a synonym for 'north', for instance at Caesar *BGall.* 4.20.1.[52]

In all these cases, the indicators pointed in a general direction and were not precise. They thus served navigators and travellers, rather than surveyors or theoretical makers of accurate maps. But even for the former, when fog or clouds covered the sky and hid the relevant astronomical bodies (the sun during the day, the moon and stars at night), there was no reliable, objective way to establish direction. This was a problem in particular for mariners, who had trouble orienting themselves in the open sea

---

[49] See also Nakassis (2004).
[50] For example in Hdt.1.6, 4.8; Thuc. 2.96; Polyb. 1.42.5, 2.14.4. The parallel Latin term for 'south' was *meridies*: e.g. Cato, *Agr.* 1.3.
[51] For example in Hdt. 1.82, 2.8; Thuc. 6.2.
[52] In Ancient Egypt and in the Bible, details of local topography and geography were used to indicate direction, for instance up-river or down-river, toward the sea, toward the Negev. In other pre-modern societies in East Asia and America, directions were sometimes indicated by colours.

without topographic landmarks, and who thus generally preferred coastal routes.

The final means of identifying a site – after stating its relative position, its distance from a particular reference point, and the direction from there in which it lay – was by its name and a short identifier, describing, for example, the quality of the harbour, peculiar topographic features, a local commodity or an ethnographic trait.

The combination of all these orientating elements enabled a more precise determination of location, even if it was not entirely accurate. All five features – order, distance, direction, toponym, and local traits – were used throughout antiquity, but gradually gained a more objective character. This progress towards an increasingly reliable and definite system came about through the introduction of standards and of instruments to measure distance and direction. Greek and Roman methods for measuring distance have been already introduced (3.1). It remains to show how direction and more exact coordinates came to be determined.

This issue introduces the connection between astronomy and geography, for ancient astronomers made fundamental contributions to fixing coordinates on the globe, in particular by the combination of intersecting lines of latitude and longitude.

Systematic mathematical analysis of theories and observations began in the Hellenistic period, and specifically with Eratosthenes, who was based in Ptolemaic Alexandria. In addition to his major contribution to the calculation of the circumference of the earth (3.1), Eratosthenes recorded data for the fixing of lines on the globe that resulted in a basic grid on which the *oikoumenê* was, at least mentally, drawn. Dicaearchus of Messana refined some of his predecessor's notions. But it was the astronomer Hipparchus of Nicaea (*c.* 190–126 BCE) who significantly advanced the discussion, mainly in his *Against the Geography of Eratosthenes*, parts of which are preserved in Strabo's *Geography*.[53] The outcome of his research formed the basis for the theories and data in Ptolemy's *Geography* and *Almagest*.

How then did astronomy overlap with geography? The basic idea was to observe the change in the size of shadows cast by objects at different points on the globe. This was a reflection of the differing position of the sun in relation to the earth, which created different angles of its rays in different locations. Thus, the relative size of shadows made it possible to calculate one's position on the globe. Because of its accuracy, a *gnômôn*

---

[53] Dicks (1960).

(sundial) was used for such calculations on the same day, and specifically on a day that could be defined astronomically, the equinox:[54]

The shadow of the *gnômôn* at the equinox is of one magnitude at Athens, another at Alexandria, another at Rome, and is different in Placentia and in other parts of the world. (Vitr. *De arch.* 9.1.1)

Another means of calculation, also connected to the relative position of the sun and the earth, involved the different length of days in different places on earth. The measurement of shadows and the observation of different day-lengths thus became the basis of a systematic idea of latitudes – lines or regions stretching from east to west across the globe, parallel to the equator. The equator (*isêmerion* in Greek; *aequinoctialis circulus* in Latin) was an imaginary line on the earth's surface at a point where (as the name indicates) day and night were of equal duration. The equator was equidistant from both poles, and divided the earth into northern and southern hemispheres. Latitudes (*parallêloi* in Greek) were mental lines parallel to the equator, each situated in a specific angle in relation to the sun. As a result, weather conditions in various latitude zones were assumed to be different. Modern astronomy asserts that the sun may be at its zenith[55] only on points on the globe situated between 23º latitude north or south (the Tropics of Cancer and Capricorn, respectively), and that midnight sun is possible only north or south of latitude 66º in both hemispheres.

As noted, geographical latitude could be measured by observation of several astronomical phenomena, all connected:[56]

1 the rising and setting time of the sun and certain constellations which, due to their angular position in relation to the globe, are similar for sites situated on the same parallel. Such observations are most easily made at the solstice (in summer, on 20/21 June; in winter, on 21/22 December), when the tilt of the earth is most inclined towards or away from the sun (that is, the longest and shortest days of the year);[57]

2 the angle between the sun's position above the horizon and the earth's surface. This was either estimated by simple observation or, better,

---

[54] Evans (1998), 27–31, 59–63.

[55] Zenith = a point situated vertically and directly above a specific location.

[56] Diller (1934); one can also measure along the longitude the distance between sites whose latitude is known, for example, the equator.

[57] The Greeks used equinoctial hours in their astronomical calculations. Because the length of hours (measured by dividing daylight into 12 equal parts) changed seasonally, a fixed hour length would be set as the one measured at the equinox (that is, on days when day and night are equal in length: 20/21 March and 22/23 September).

calculated by measuring the ratio between the size of a *gnômôn* and the size of the shadow it cast at noon on the summer solstice; identical results for different places meant that they were situated on the same latitude;

3 the changing proportion between the durations of day and night.

All three factors depended on the observer's position on the globe, and changed when the observer moved south or north, that is latitudinally. These measurements enabled an observer to calculate his distance from the equator, provided he had a figure for the circumference of the globe. In all cases, the geographical parallels were to some extent theoretical, because it was impossible to measure them with absolute accuracy.

Pytheas of Massalia, who made a pioneering journey to northern Europe (2.3), observed the changing length of the day as he travelled north, and accompanied his observations with indications of the height of the sun above the horizon. Hipparchus took these data and calculated latitudes with them. For example, Pytheas read the ratio of a *gnômôn* to its shadow at Massalia at noon on the summer solstice as 120:41.8. This gives an angle of 19°12', which translates into a latitude of about 43°, very near the truth (43°18'0" N). Soon a system of parallels was created, which influenced the overall perception of the *oikoumenê*:

The parallel through the mouth of the Borysthenes [modern Dnieper] is conjectured by Hipparchus and others to be the same as that through Britain, from the fact that the parallel through Byzantium is the same as that through Massalia. For as to the relation of the *gnômôn* to the shadow, which Pytheas has given to Massalia, Hipparchus says he observed this same relation in Byzantium at the same time of the year as that mentioned by Pytheas. (Strabo 1.4.4)

The standard way to report latitude was by measuring the duration of the longest day of the year. 'All such phenomena are obvious to the eye even of a layman and do not require mathematical notation' (Strabo 2.1.18). Since the Greeks and Romans used equinoctial hours (see note 57, above), they could have a comparative standard only when measuring sunlight hours on the longest day:

the longest day covers $12^8/_9$ equinoctial hours at Meroe, but 14 hours at Alexandria, 15 in Italy, and 17 in Britain. (Plin. *HN* 2.186)

The result is apparent, for example, in the charts of Ptolemy, which were intended to provide a basis for a graphic map:

The first parallel differing from [the equator's twelve hours] by ¼ hour and distant by 4¼° as established approximately by geometrical demonstrations; the second, differing by ½ hour … the fourth, differing by 1 hour … and drawn through Meroe [Ethiopia] … the tenth, differing by 2½ hours and distant 36° and drawn through Rhodes … the twenty-first, differing by 8 hours and distant 63°, which is drawn through Thule … and the parallel that marks the southern limit will also be drawn; it is as far south of the equator as the parallel through Meroe is north of it. (*Geog.* 1.23)[58]

According to this scheme, the inhabited region of the world begins in the fourth Ptolemaic parallel or latitude (at Meroe), and ends in the twenty-first, which runs through Thule. These two lines are the borders of the *oikoumenê* as it was known at Ptolemy's time, Ethiopia in the south, and the Shetlands in the north.

But there are some variations in this basic system of latitudes (which is still accepted today). Dicaearchus of Messana, for example, established a central latitude different from the equator. His idea was to place this major mental line not in the centre of the globe, which interested astronomers more than geographers, but in the centre of the *oikoumenê*, which was held to be situated only in the northern hemisphere:

Dicaearchus divides the earth not by waters, but by a straight line from the Pillars through Sardinia, Sicily, Peloponnese, Ionia, Caria, Lycia, Pamphylia, Cilicia and Taurus, up to the mountains of Imaus (Himalayas). And he names the north and the south in relation to these places. (Agathemerus, *Sketch of Geography*, 5)[59]

By inventing the latitude 'zero', Dicaearchus promoted the notion that the Mediterranean was at the centre of the spherical earth.[60] Eratosthenes expanded Dicaearchus' concept, by adding a series of five additional parallels.[61] For these measurements, particularly for the northern latitudes, he relied on the astronomical observations of Pytheas of Massalia in the north. These Eratosthenian latitudes were inherited by Hipparchus and eventually by Ptolemy (in the *Almagest*).

Hipparchus shaped basic observational methods (shadows and daylight) into an accurate system. He subdivided Eratosthenes' figure for the circumference of the earth (252,000 *stadia*) into 360°, and established parallel strips of 700 *stadia*.[62] Moreover, his system of latitudes extended over the entire globe, including regions beyond the range of observation.

---

[58] Ptolemy's quotations are based on the translation by Berggren and Jones (2000).
[59] Diller (1975), 61.
[60] Heidel (1976), 111–113; Keyser (2001), 365–368.
[61] Shcheglov (2006).
[62] Shcheglov (2005). Only in the mid-second century BCE did Greek astronomers adopt the 360° system from the Babylonians; see Lewis (2001), 40–41.

Eratosthenes relied only on observations from accessible sites, which limited his range of latitudes. But Hipparchus relied on calculation and could therefore produce data for unseen places as well. Because of the larger span of his theoretical latitudes, Hipparchus could expand Eratosthenes' five major parallels to compose a grid covering the entire globe. But even in Ptolemy's time, this idea remained theoretical. Hipparchus' calculations were probably the basis for Ptolemy's lists, which also expressed latitude in degrees. But the expression of parallels through day-length (i.e., in units of hours) was retained until the Renaissance simply for the sake of consistency with the classical tradition.

Latitudes defined the position of sites on the globe in reference to only one parameter. For a more accurate determination, longitudes or meridians were needed as well:

Meridian circles are circles drawn through the poles of the universe and through the point which is above the head of any individual standing on the earth. The poles are the same for all these circles, but the vertical point is different for different individuals. Hence we can draw an infinite number of meridian circles. (Cleomedes, *On Orbits of Celestial Bodies* 1.10)[63]

These meridian circles, or longitudes, are scientifically defined as the angular distance on the earth east or west of the prime meridian, and are measured in degrees. Today the prime meridian, assigned the value 0°, is in Greenwich, England. In antiquity, the prime meridian as defined by Ptolemy was in the Blessed Isles (the Canary Islands), and the set of longitudes stretched east to this line to cover the *oikoumenê* (but not the entire globe).

From theory to practice: longitude can be measured by calculating the time difference between two points situated relatively east or west of one another, accounting for the movement of the sun across the sky. In antiquity, there was no practical means to fix longitude because there was no way to measure the precise time simultaneously in different places. The Greeks therefore used travel data and guessed distances along latitudes. Eratosthenes' system, which was based on travel estimates, featured a major meridian passing from south to north: Meroe–Byzantium–Borysthenes. Although Eratosthenes was aware that this line was imprecise, he treated it as straight. Even Hipparchus could not determine longitude, although he knew the theoretical means to do so (i.e., the difference in time between places):

---

[63] Bowen and Todd (2004).

The victory of Alexander the Great is said to have caused an eclipse of the moon at Arbela [in modern northern Iraq] at the second hour of the night, while the same eclipse in Sicily occurred when the moon was just rising. An eclipse of the sun, that occurred the day before the Kalends of May in the consulship of Vipstanus and Fonteius a few years ago, was visible in Campania between the seventh and eighth hours of the day, but reported by Corbulo commanding in Armenia as observed between the tenth and eleventh hours: this was because the curve of the globe discloses and hides different phenomena for different localities. If the earth were flat, all would be visible to all alike at the same time. (Plin. *HN* 2.180)

The eclipse in Alexander's time was observed in Arbela and in Carthage with a three-hour difference in time, which translated into 45° of longitude. Hipparchus knew this, but thought that this method was not sufficiently accurate. He planned to establish a complete grid based on accurate mathematical calculations, not mere estimates, but the project was never completed.

In addition to the division of the inhabited world into continents, which was clearly, if somewhat controversially, made on the basis of natural considerations (3.1), Eratosthenes initiated several attempts to offer other sub-divisions, probably with a view to producing a graphic map of the world (chapter 4). He divided the *oikoumenê* into four parts, by creating two intersecting major lines of latitude and longitude. For this latitude, he chose the meridian through Alexandria, Rhodes and Caria, creating an east–west division. He then envisioned the Mediterranean, the Taurus range and the Ganges River as points on a straight line, creating a north–south division as well.[64] Another idea was notionally to cut up the landmass into random squares, which Eratosthenes called 'seals' (*sphragides*).

The most accurate way to find a point on the globe is to indicate the intersection of latitude and longitude (i.e., to give an orthogonal pair of coordinates). Today, the global positioning system (GPS) supplies accurate information of this sort, but in antiquity the necessary data were obtained from indications of longitude (in degrees) and latitude (in hours of the longest day, or in degrees). Using these two parameters, Ptolemy could offer a list of thousands of toponyms with their coordinates. These were not actually observed or measured for each point separately, but were calculated through the distance over the ground from better-known places, themselves often inaccurately fixed. Ptolemy's main goal in his *Geography* was to offer a series of tables with accurate lists of numerical

[64] Dilke (1985), 55–66.

coordinates of sites, as a basis for a graphic map (chapter 4).[65] The work was accordingly arranged as follows: Book 1, a summary of the technical problems of mapping a sphere on a plane surface; Books 2–7, an extensive list of coordinates of sites; Book 8, a description of the resulting maps. Here is an example of the list of locations related to Gallia Lugdunensis (*Geog.* 2.8):

After the mouths of the river Liger:

Brivates	17⅔	48¾
Mouths of river Herius	17	49¼
Vidana	16½	49⅔
Cape Gabaeum	15¼	49¾

Ptolemy thus marked geographical features expressed as points, for example cities, river mouths and mountain peaks, and refrained from indicating linear features such as coasts, borders, river channels and mountain chains. The system could also be translated into distances:

We can obtain other terrestrial distances without measuring them, even if they are not direct or aligned with a meridian or parallel, provided we carefully observe the angle [of the distance to the meridian] and the meridian altitude at the termini. To repeat: if we know the ratio between the greatest circle and the arc subtended by the distance, the number of *stadia* can easily be calculated from the known circumference of the earth. (Ptol. *Geog.* 1.3.3)

This grid also allowed a more scientific definition of the situation of the *oikoumenê* on the globe:

[Its] greatest breadth is represented by the line that runs through the Nile, a line that begins at the parallel that runs through the cinnamon-producing country and the island of the fugitive Egyptians, and ends at the parallel through Ierne. Its length is represented by the line drawn perpendicular to it which runs from the west through the Pillars and the Strait of Sicily to Rhodes and the Gulf of Issus; passes along the Taurus range, which encircles Asia; and ends at the Eastern Sea between India and the country of those Scythians who live beyond Bactriana ... Accordingly we must conceive of a parallelogram. (Strabo 2.5.14)

The concept of a theoretical grid on the globe was directly associated with attempts to produce graphic representations of the world. We accordingly turn now to cartography in antiquity.

---

[65] Riley (1995), esp. 230–236; Berggren and Jones (2000).

CHAPTER 4

Cartography

Kai Brodersen

4.1 A PRE-MODERN WORLD

In 1986, seven maps drawn in ink on thin pieces of wood were discovered in the grave of a military officer buried around 239 BCE; the maps represent a small region at a scale of *c.* 1:300,000. Already in 1973, the excavation of the grave of a ruler of 168 BCE had brought to light a map of a larger region; on it, drawn to a scale of *c.* 1:180,000, were marked plains, mountains, rivers, roads and places with standardized symbols and names. The same grave preserved another map, which presented a detail of the same region, at a scale *c.* 1:100,000, marking forts and lines of defence. During their lifetimes, the officer and the ruler had both apparently had access to scale maps that were so important to them that they were buried with them. We also have literary evidence from the same period of the use of maps. A historical work from the second/first century BCE, for example, relates that in 227 BCE the son of a ruler ordered a man to kill a neighbouring dynast. To get close to his intended victim, the killer pretended to want to offer the dynast a map sent to him as a present by his master. He gained access to the man and was able to conceal a dagger in the map roll. But the victim survived and founded his own dynasty. Twenty years later, in 207 BCE, his capital was attacked, and, although the soldiers could have ransacked the palace and looted its treasures, they were interested only in the administrative centre with its archive and its maps – which ultimately contributed to the formation of a new dynasty that lasted until 9 CE.[1]

The pre-modern world[2] to which these artefacts and stories belong is not that of Greece and Rome. Rather, the events described above took place in ancient China; there are no comparable examples from the ancient Mediterranean. Is this lack of evidence from the classical world merely a

[1] 239 BCE: Yee (1994), 37f.; 168 BCE: Bulling (1978); Hsu (1978); (1984); stories: Watson (1961), 125f.; cf. Brodersen (2003), 139f.
[2] Raaflaub and Talbert (2010).

coincidence? Or is it a consequence of a feature of pre-modern Europe, in which 'high culture' forms only a thin 'veneer', as Patricia Crone argues in her study of (non-classical) pre-industrial societies:

An educated man could travel over huge distances speaking the same learned language, discussing the same body of ideas … But the trans-local culture did not penetrate very deep … The high culture owed this peculiar combination of wide expanse and superficiality to the nature of communications in the pre-industrial world, in combination with scarcity and political factors.[3]

These characteristics can be observed in the Greco-Roman world as well. As was demonstrated in previous chapters, ancient 'educated men' covered 'huge distances' in both place and time to debate scientific questions about geography. They communicated in the same 'learned language' – Greek – and discussed 'the same body of ideas'. Their debate 'did not penetrate very deep' within the culture, which is why the preceding chapters draw a sharp distinction between descriptive geography, with its wide application, and mathematical or scientific geography, for which no such application was envisaged or achieved. The reasons for this divide include the limited quantity of scientific geographic scholarship, the 'nature of communications' and 'scarcity and political factors'. All this is also evident in the history of cartography (a modern term created via a combination of Greek *chartês*, 'chart', and *graphein*, 'write' or 'draw'), that is, the study of maps as a special form of communicating geographic knowledge. Maps are generally two-dimensional representations, often to scale, of portions of the earth's surface. What do we know about ancient cartography?

It must be said at the outset that we have little contemporary evidence for Greco-Roman maps. In the modern world, the nature of communications allows original texts and graphics to be preserved, transmitted and accessed for extended periods of time. The pre-modern world, on the other hand, had only a series of copies to work with, made over the centuries on organic material. The process was almost manageable for texts, multiple copies of which could be created by copyist teams working from dictation. But it was not feasible for graphics, the copying of which inevitably led to increasing distortion. Copies of copies of copies must generally have been very different from the vanished original, hence the scarcity of scholarly illustrations transmitted from the ancient world.[4]

Methods for accurately reproducing and eventually printing maps in sufficient quantities to enable cartographical knowledge to 'penetrate very

[3] Crone (1989), 88–89.   [4] Stückelberger (1994).

deep' are in fact a feature only of modern times. Gutenberg's invention of moving type did not lead to the multiplication of maps. Only Senefelder's invention of lithography in 1796, and the innovative use of it for the mass printing of graphics, including in colour, in the century that followed, allowed maps to be printed and distributed in quantity. This allowed general access to accurate maps and led, *inter alia*, to the introduction of geography as a school subject; the invention of the school atlas in the late nineteenth century; and the deep penetration of cartographic information to almost all members of industrial societies from the late nineteenth century on. Any assumption that maps were widely available in the pre-industrial world thus derives from anachronistic thinking based on later developments.

It is nonetheless the case that many modern school atlases could not (and cannot) resist the temptation to reconstruct ancient maps by combining modern knowledge about the shape of the earth's landmass with data from ancient texts. The nineteenth century in particular saw many such reconstructions,[5] but even the most recent grand atlas of the ancient world, which accompanies the *Neue Pauly* encyclopaedia,[6] presents supposed reconstructions of the world maps of Hecataeus, Herodotus, Eratosthenes and Ptolemy. Such reconstructions introduce a host of unwanted modern concepts into the ancient data: north is on top, for example; the shape of coastlines for which no ancient descriptions are available is the familiar modern one (e.g., Italy reconstructed in the shape of a boot – a modern idea unknown in the ancient world),[7] or colour is used to mark the continents and the sea. There is no evidence for the use of such forms of representation in ancient maps, and this book deliberately presents no such reconstructions.

There is even a temptation to go beyond reconstructions and invent – that is, falsify – maps from the ancient world. Every generation or so, a new 'discovery' of such a map is announced, only to be exposed as either a hoax designed to embarrass an individual scholar or scholars in general, or an attempt to make money from an unsuspecting public. 'The earliest Greek map to come down to us in any form and the first physical relief map known'[8] was 'discovered' in 1967 on Ionian coins of the fourth century BCE (increasing their market value in modern collectors'

---

[5] E.g. Smith and Grove (1872); Bunbury (1883); Sieglin (1893); Miller (1898).
[6] Wittke *et al.* (2007), 4–5, and (2009), 4–5, while acknowledging the problem of reconstructions, continue to present such maps.
[7] Bertrand (1989).   [8] Johnston (1967).

circles). But the fact is that the design on such coins varies and probably only shows waves and perhaps sea monsters; even the discoverer of these maps later doubted that they could be interpreted as such.[9] The 'oldest original world map'[10] was 'found' on a gold coin dating to the time of the emperor Augustus that supposedly represented Europe, Asia and Africa; it was later exposed as a fake.[11] 'The oldest geographic map ever discovered in Europe',[12] on a sherd 'found' in 2005, allegedly presenting a map of the heel of Italy, was similarly soon shown to be a hoax intended to embarrass a prominent archaeologist.[13] The same was true of a plan of the Roman settlement at Aguntum 'found' during excavations in 1976,[14] and soon exposed as a practical joke by the excavator's disgruntled students.[15] Likewise 'one of the few surviving geographical maps of the pre-Augustan period' (there are in fact none), a piece of sandstone shaped like Gaul (or modern-day France) supposedly found near a fort used by Julius Caesar and immediately published in the monumental *History of Cartography*,[16] was eventually unmasked as a hoax.[17] It is probably the desire of modern scholars to find tangible evidence for the existence of maps in the ancient world that has led to embarrassing credulity vis-à-vis such hoaxes and fakes.

4.2 DESCRIPTIVE AND SCIENTIFIC CARTOGRAPHY

While there are no remains of Greek or Roman scientific maps, some plans of small plots of land, drawn to scale, are preserved. Ancient building plans usually apply a very large scale (if not outright 1:1),[18] and it was of course possible to measure existing structures and represent their topographical relationships on a plan. Several such large-scale plans of tombs along the Via Appia are preserved.[19] The most spectacular plan of this kind is the so-called *Forma Urbis Romae* (a modern name), a plan of the centre of Rome created around 200 CE, more than a thousand fragments of which survive.[20] The *Forma* lacks a uniform scale and

---

[9] Dilke (1988), 92.   [10] Miller (1895), 131.   [11] Brodersen (2003), 77.
[12] Gomarasca (2009), 21, in a chapter on 'milestones in the history of cartography'.
[13] Yntema (2006); Brodersen (2010), 835.
[14] Alzinger (1977).   [15] Brein (1980).
[16] Dilke (1987), 207 with fig.   [17] Brodersen (2003), 143.
[18] Haselberger (1994) and (forthcoming).
[19] Heisel (1993).
[20] Cf. http://formaurbis.stanford.edu with bibliography (accessed 4 July 2011). For a recent interpretation, see Trimble (2007). A similar, but unrelated fragment was published in 1984: Conticello de' Spagnolis (1984), 15, fig. 7.

orientation;[21] most likely many individual plans were combined to create an impressive display of the topography of the inner city of Rome.

In flat territory with few buildings, surveyors' instruments allowed straight lines and right angles to be plotted on the land itself.[22] Agricultural land, typically in territory created afresh by floods (a regular occurrence in the Nile delta), or acquired through colonization or conquest, could thus be divided, and taxation or ownership recorded. Such records were usually texts that assigned every plot of land (*centuria*) a unique identifier, by recording its distance from the *decumanus* and the *cardo* lines, which formed a rectangular cross at the centre of the territory:

Of the 35th *centuria* right of the *decumanus* and the 47th beyond the *cardo* (there are) for Lucius Terebintius, son of Lucius, of the Tribus Pollia 66⅔ *iugera*, for Gaius Numisius, son of Gaius, from the Tribus Sellatina 66⅔ *iugera*, and for Publius Tarquinius, son of Gnaeus, from the Tribus Terentina 66⅔ *iugera*. (Hyginus Gromaticus, *Constitutio limitum*, p. 201 Lachmann; p. 164 Thulin)

Recording the position of such a plot of land on a plan has no immediate functional advantage over a text, but can be used to visualize the relative position of individual plots. A small bronze plaque from Lacimurga in Spain, published in 1990,[23] shows such a visualization, and demonstrates that the concept of scale is irrelevant for this type of record: the individual plots of land all measure CCLXXV (275) units, as the inscribed text shows, but are displayed in widely differing shapes and sizes (see figure 3).

At Arausio (Orange) in France, the local distribution of *centuriae* was displayed in several large inscriptions which put the individual plots in their correct topographic position on a plan (not to scale) and also gave their individual locations in the form 'right/left of the *decumanus* and hither/thither of the *cardo*'.[24]

As for mapping regions rather than small plots of land, towns or centuriations, space that could be traversed on sea or land by soldiers, traders, ambassadors or pilgrims was typically represented by lines following such routes, the *periplous* and the *itinerarium* being the regular method of representing these routes as text. Graphic forms of the *periplous* and the itinerary, on the other hand, are rare. The few extant examples belong to contexts where representation and display were envisaged. A list of stations on the land-route from Gades (Cadiz) to Rome adorns

---

[21] Brodersen (2003), 235.   [22] Campbell (1996); (2000).
[23] Sáez Fernández (1990), 207. The fragment measures 8.6 by 5.6 cm. For the differences between such plans and the topographical reality cf. Cuomo (2007), 109.
[24] *CIL* XII 1244; Piganiol (1962).

Figure 3: Recording of position of land plots on a bronze
plaque from Lacimurga, Spain; *AE* 1990, 529. After Sáez
Fernández, (1990), 207, by kind permission of Pedro Sáez Fernandez.

four second-century CE silver beakers,[25] and soldiers who had served on
Hadrian's Wall in Britain presented a list of the names of stations along
the wall above a graphic image of a crenellated wall (see figure 4).[26]

Some stations along the Black Sea coast are depicted on a unique circular leather object – perhaps a ceremonial shield – dating to the third
century CE and found in Dura Europos.[27] The authenticity, in whole or
part, of the recently published first-century CE Artemidorus Papyrus,
which combines geographic texts, a diagrammatic and apparently unfin-
ished map (it lacks toponyms), and images of animals and human body
parts (see 2.3) is still being discussed,[28] as is its potential to contribute to
the history of cartography.[29] Much better known is the so-called *Tabula
Peutingeriana*, an essentially diagrammatic representation, not to scale,
of the topographical relationship of stations along routes in the later
Roman Empire. The *Tabula* combines a route diagram with toponyms

---

[25] *CIL* XI 3281–3284.
[26] See also *AE* 1950, 56 [Amiens], *CIL* VII 1291 = *RIB* II 2, 2415.53 [Rudge], *Britannia* 2004, 344
[Staffordshire Moorlands].
[27] *Dura Parchment* 9 = *AE* 1925, 123 = Codex Paris suppl. gr. 1354² v, cf. Cumont (1926), I 261 ff.;
Arnaud (1989).
[28] Gallazzi *et al.* (2008); cf. Brodersen and Elsner (2009).
[29] Cf. Beard (2006), I: 'It seems pretty clear that it was a rather dull route-plan of some area of
Spain (which area is not entirely certain), marking major roads and rivers, places along them and
the distances between. It is not, in other words, what people have called the "missing link" in
ancient cartography, the start of map-making in the modern sense.'

•꓃·ᴍꓥꟷꟷꓘꓥꓐ ꓥꞮꞮ ꓥ∨꓃꓅ⴹꞮꞮ ꝋꝺꝠ꓀ꓵꓷ꓅Ꝋ Ꮆꓥ꓅ꓐꝋ Ꮆ꓃ꓥ Ꝡ ꓡꓐꓥꝤꓥꝤꓥ•

Figure 4: A list of names of stations above an image of a wall, *RIB* ii 2, 2415.53. After S.S. Frere and R.S.O. Tomlin, *The Roman Inscriptions of Britain*, vol. 2.2, Stroud and Wolfeboro Falls, 1991, 56, by kind permission of the Trustees of the Haverfield Bequest.

and information on distances, as well as graphic elements. What is preserved is a twelfth-century manuscript (owned by the humanist Peutinger in the sixteenth century, hence its name); as we lack classical parallels, we cannot draw conclusions about the appearance of the possible ancient exemplar, although it has been plausibly argued that the *Tabula* is a copy of a late Roman map of similar appearance.[30]

Both plans of plots of land, towns or *centuriae*, and regional maps visualize data that descriptive geography regularly presents only in texts to be used in everyday contexts. For the largest areas covered by maps, the continents of the *oikoumenê*, or even the entire globe, descriptive geography is of no immediate use. A scene in Aristophanes' *Clouds* (originally produced in Athens in 423 BCE), in which the rustic Strepsiades (S), converses with a disciple (D) of the learned Socrates, makes this point:

s (discovering a variety of mathematical instruments): Why, what is this, in the name of heaven? Tell me.
D: This is Astronomy.
s: But what is this?
D: Geometry.
s: What then is the use of this?
D: To measure out the land.
s: Land that belongs to an allotment?
D: No, but the whole earth.
s: You tell me a clever notion; for the contrivance is democratic and useful.

---

[30] Cf. most recently Talbert (2010), *contra* Albu (2005).

D: See, here's a *periodos* of the whole earth. Do you see? This is Athens.

S: What say you? I don't believe you; for I do not see the Dicasts sitting.

D: Be assured that this is truly the territory of Athens.

S: Why, where are my fellow-tribesmen of Cicynna?

D: Here they are. And Euboea here, as you see, is stretched out a long way by the side of it to a great distance.

S: I know that; for it was stretched by us and Pericles. But where is Lacedaemon?

D: Where is it? Here it is.

S: How near it is to us! Pay great attention to this, to remove it very far from us.

D: By Zeus, it is not possible.

S: Then you will weep for it. (Aristophanes, *Clouds* 200ff., trans. W.J. Hickie, adapted)

Strepsiades is only familiar with maps representing an allotment, while the disciple presents a *periodos*, a graphic representation of the world, to which he has exclusive access in the learned environment of Socrates' school. Maps are thus mentioned in a scholarly context, although we have no way of knowing what they looked like at this point. Nor can we tell what the *periodos* in question was made of; whether it was (at least roughly) to scale; how coastlines, areas cities and their territory (such as 'territory of Athens' and Lacedaemon (Sparta)), and places (such as Cicynna) were represented; and whether the map also showed rivers, mountain ranges, landmarks and roads.

As it happens, Theophrastus (a student of Aristotle, who was in turn a student of Plato, who was in turn a student of Socrates) is said to have mentioned in his will 'tables on which the *periodoi* of the world are' (Diogenes Laertius 5.51), an anecdote demonstrating both the uniqueness and the value of such maps, and the fact that – in Crone's words (see above) – 'an educated man could travel over huge distances' also of time, 'speaking the same learned language, discussing the same body of ideas'.

Socrates' disciple invites us into the realm of scientific cartography. Thinking about the shape of the world, and about ways to represent the results of such deliberations in a graphic form, is known from the beginning of Greek ethnography and historiography. Herodotus, for instance, writes:

I laugh when I see how many have before now written *periodoi gês*, not one of them giving a reasonable account; for they describe the world as round as if fashioned by compasses, and encircled by the Ocean, and Asia and Europe as of a like size. For myself, I will in a few words indicate the extent of the two, and how each should be drawn. (Hdt. 4.36.2)

Chapter 3 discussed the evidence for scientific geography, including the use of graphic forms of presenting and interpreting data. None of the maps referred to in the literature is preserved, and modern reconstructions (see above) necessarily rely on assumptions unsupported by ancient evidence. The most substantial collection of data designed to allow construction of a map, along with instructions about how to draw it, is in the work of Claudius Ptolemaeus (Ptolemy)[31] in the second century CE (3.2). The earliest preserved maps based on his data, on the other hand, date from a millennium later.

4.3 MAPS IN THE SERVICE OF THE STATE?

Finally, were there 'maps in the service of the state', as a chapter heading in the monumental *History of Cartography* has it?[32] A story reported in Herodotus appears to suggest this:

It was in the reign of Cleomenes that Aristagoras the tyrant of Miletus came to Sparta. When he had an audience with the king, as the Lacedaemonians report, he brought with him a bronze tablet on which a *periodos* of all the earth was engraved, and all the sea and all the rivers … 'The lands in which they dwell lie next to each other, as I shall show: next to the Ionians here are the Lydians, who inhabit a good land and have great store of silver.' This he said pointing to the *periodos* of the earth which he had brought engraved on the tablet. 'Next to the Lydians,' said Aristagoras, 'you see the Phrygians here, the Eastern ones, men that of all known to me are the richest in flocks and in the fruits of the earth. Close by them are the Cappadocians, whom we call Syrians, and their neighbours are the Cilicians, whose land reaches to the sea here, in which you see this island of Cyprus lying. The yearly tribute which they pay to the king is five hundred talents. Next to the Cilicians are here the Armenians, another people rich in flocks, and after them the Armenians, the Matieni, whose country I show you. After them there is the Cissia land, in which, on the Choaspes, lies Susa here, where the great king lives and where the storehouses of his wealth are located.' … When, on the day appointed for the answer, they came to the place upon which they had agreed, Cleomenes asked Aristagoras how many days' journey it was from the Ionian Sea to the king. (Hdt. 5.49.1–50.1)

In 499 BCE, the ruler of Miletus, Aristagoras, used a *periodos* of the whole world to persuade the Spartan (Lacedaemonian) king Cleomenes to join Miletus in a war against the King of Persia. Herodotus' story represents Aristagoras as pointing to the tablet repeatedly ('here', 'this' place, etc.), but goes beyond what seems to be marked on it in explaining the

---

[31] Stückelberger (2007). [32] Dilke (1987).

affluence of individual peoples. The *periodos* used by Aristagoras is irre-
trievably lost; all we know is that it was engraved on a bronze tablet and
represented lands and the peoples who inhabited them, the sea and the
island of Cyprus within it, and the city of Susa. Nor can we tell whether
it was at least roughly to scale, or how coastlines, areas and cities were
represented, or whether it showed rivers, mountain ranges, landmarks and
roads. What is remarkable for our purposes, however, is that Aristagoras
does not use the graphic image to explain more than a list would have
allowed, and that neither does the Spartan king understand more than
that; his reply refers to the *periodos* as if it had been an itinerary, when he
inquires about the overall distance to be covered – and as a consequence
declines to join the Milesian's march on Susa.

As for maps intended for representational use 'in the service of the
state', newly conquered space was regularly presented in triumphal processions, not by way of maps, however, but by means of inscriptions listing the conquests, or exhibits such as captives, animals and treasures.[33]
Agrippa, the right-hand man of the Roman emperor Augustus, is often
credited with a celebrated artefact: a map of the world displayed in the
centre of Rome. In his influential study of *The Power of Images in the Age
of Augustus*, Paul Zanker writes:

> Those with time on their hands could also contemplate the map of the world
> which was commissioned by Agrippa and later transferred to the Porticus
> Vipsaniae. It was intended to give the Roman people an idea of 'their' empire
> and heighten their awareness of being *princeps terrarum populus* (Livy, Praef.).
> We need only think of the impressive marble plan of the Imperium Romanum
> which Mussolini had placed on the ancient ruins along the Via del Impero.[34]

However, we have no clear knowledge about this map. Unlike the five
maps Mussolini had engraved in 1936 on large marble plates to show the
growth of the Roman Empire and the recent Italian conquest of Ethiopia
(the latter map has since been removed), nothing remains of Agrippa's
map. There is no evidence for its physical appearance, forcing scholars
to speculate about its shape. It has variously been described as a globe, a
flat map executed as a mosaic, a painting and engraved bronze or marble.[35] Its shape has been presented as circular, oval and rectangular.[36] Its

---

[33] Östenberg (2009) and 1.3.   [34] Zanker (1988), 143.

[35] Globe: Levi (1987), 17; painting: Urlichs (1876), 8; mosaic: Ritschl (1877), 768; engraving: Torelli (1982), 120.

[36] Circular: Mommsen (1908), 306; oval: Kiessling (1914), 891; rectangular: Kubtischek (1919), 2110; Bowersock (1983), 167.

size has been described as 6–10 metres high; 9 metres wide by 18 metres high; 24 metres wide and, on top of a 5 metre base, 12 metres high (the scholar in question added that experts assured him that viewers who are not short-sighted would be able to make out details at that height); or 75 metres wide but only 4.5 metres high.[37] As for orientation, east, south and north have all been assumed to have been on top,[38] while as for design, the map has been taken to resemble the *Tabula Peutingeriana*, a medieval *Mappamundi*, and an early modern portolan map.[39] Such wildly incompatible opinions demonstrate the difficulty of imagining a map of the world on display in Augustan Rome. We might even wonder whether there was a map at all, since all ancient references to the display are compatible with the assumption that what Agrippa presented was merely an inscription offering some geographical detail.[40] Augustus' conquest of the Alps, after all, was celebrated by a great inscription,[41] as was the conquest of Lycia in 43 CE – with a monumental inscription (recently discovered) listing stations in the new province.[42] Perhaps Agrippa too visualized the greatness of the Empire in such an inscription. In any case, it is an anachronism to require us – as Zanker does – to 'think of the impressive marble plan of the Imperium Romanum which Mussolini had placed on the ancient ruins along the Via del Impero'.

We thus lack the sort of evidence for maps in the classical world that we have for ancient China. Arguments from silence are dangerous, since so much has been lost over the millennia. But the presentation of geographic data in *periploi* and *itineraria* (chapter 2) may well have met not only individual but also state needs. After all, maps present a host of redundant information which the user must scan and reduce to retrieve the specific material needed; witness the current general preference for itineraries provided by satellite navigation (satnav) apparatuses, which provide only convenient driving directions, over traditional roadmaps.

To sum up, the pre-modern Greco-Roman world generally managed without maps. Descriptive geography relied on texts, and even scientific discourse, which spanned wide spatial and temporal expanses, relied

---

[37] 6–10 metres: Klotz (1931), 41; 9 by 18 metres: Tierney (1962), 152; 24 by 12 metres: Müllenhoff (1875), 194; 4.5 by 75 metres: Grilli (1989), 140f.
[38] East: Miller (1898), 147; south: Partsch (1907), 1058; north: Dilke (1987), 208.
[39] *Tabula*: Mommsen (1908), 306; Bowersock (1983), 167; Talbert (2010); *Mappamundi*: Philippi (1880). Harvey (1991), 21, regards the Anglo-Saxon Cotton Map in the British Library as a 'direct descendant'. Portolan: Grosjean (1977), 18.
[40] Brodersen (2003), 273.
[41] *CIL* v 7817 (La Turbie); Pliny, *HN* 3.136.
[42] Sahin and Adak (2007) and chapter 5.

primarily on texts that could be copied and re-copied far more accurately than graphic representations of space could be. As in other pre-modern societies discussed by Patricia Crone (see above), the 'trans-local culture' of geographical science 'did not penetrate very deep'. Dissemination of scientific knowledge to a wider audience was unnecessary, and was not achieved. Scholarly debates about geography remained as little understood by a wider audience as Aristagoras' *periodos* was by Cleomenes, or as the *periodos* of Socrates' disciple was by Strepsiades. The ancient discovery of steam power did not lead to the use of steam engines, and scientific knowledge of cartography did not create maps 'in the service of the state' which could easily be understood. We cannot help but wonder what the result of a more active approach to the dissemination of scientific knowledge might have been.

CHAPTER 5

Geography in practice

5.1 THE CONNECTION BETWEEN EXPERIENCE AND TEXT

Throughout classical antiquity, people travelled. Men sailed for commercial purposes and on coasting voyages around the Mediterranean; officials travelled by land for administrative purposes at the time of the high Roman Empire; pilgrims made their way to places of religious and cultural significance; wealthy intellectuals went on tourist trips to Athens or Egypt; and military expeditions, such as the Athenian force that sailed to Sicily in 415 BCE, or the Roman military expeditions to Britain (led by Caesar in 55 and 54 BCE) and to Africa (under Tiberius in 17 CE, to quell the revolt of Tacfarinas), combined land and sea travel. The movement of individuals and groups was thus varied in regard to means of transport, goals, geographical scope and, most important, the written outcome of the experiences.

The ancients, and specifically the Greeks, who were pioneers in intellectual, geographical and scientific endeavours, became acquainted with their world through travel and scientific conjectures, the results of both of which were eventually conveyed in literary form. First came travel. Greek civilization grew up in settlements on islands or near coasts around the Mediterranean, on its European, Asian and African shores and on the Black Sea coastline. This situation required constant maritime journeys to purchase and exchange goods, as well as to meet cultural and social needs. Sailing thus became an integral part of daily life and opened the route for further, planned journeys, which eventually produced an acquaintance with new regions. Naval warfare, which had begun in the late seventh century BCE, also developed in the fifth century BCE, particularly in response to the Persian invasions. These intentions required familiarity with sea-routes, harbours, coastal topography and other local details, all essential for both merchants and warriors. Travel was also undertaken, even if less often, for pilgrimage (to oracular or healing shrines), to take part in the Olympic and Pythian games, for tourism and for intellectual purposes and encounters. Land journeys too were undertaken for all these purposes, and in the time of the Roman Empire, massive military campaigns and frequent administrative traffic made use of paved routes throughout the Empire. Practical needs were common to all motivations for travel.

Need and practice supplied information, which became the initial basis for the geographical knowledge of the ancients. Travel had a reciprocal connection with geography, because it both required and supplied information. Of necessity, it became the basis for the descriptive and scientific branches of geography, for without *being* in a place one can hardly *describe* or *measure* it – let alone produce theoretical inferences such as the measurement of the circumference of the globe.

Several preconditions determined the scope of ancient sailing and influenced attempts to break new grounds in sea travel. First, the assumption, based on practical experience, that there were only three continents – Europe, Asia and Libya (Africa) – focused such attempts on exploring the extent of these land masses (3.1). Because of the common belief in an unlimited surrounding Ocean, there were no aspirations to set sail in the open sea toward the mysterious Oceanic horizon.

Second, the Mediterranean was in fact *the* sea for most inhabitants of the known world in antiquity: for the inhabitants of the northern shore of Africa, for the Greeks on the western coasts of Asia Minor, on the islands and on the Greek mainland, and for the Phoenicians.[1] Later, the same was true for the Romans who occupied these regions and saw the Mediterranean as their own sea (*mare nostrum*). The only opening to the outer sea, or Ocean, was at the Pillars of Heracles (the Straits of Gibraltar) while the straits at the Hellespont led to the smaller, but still large, closed Black Sea. Adventurous pioneering sailing expeditions were therefore mostly conducted through the western straits and then continued either south, off the coasts of Africa, or along the coast of Europe. Other, slightly later sailing expeditions focused on the southern Ocean, mainly along the sea-routes between Africa and India.

A third premise was that journeys in the open sea were dangerous even when undertaken in the inner, and nominally safer, Mediterranean. Several spots were especially known for their high risk, for example Cape Malea at the southeast tip of the Peloponnese, where constant winds and

---

[1] Plato's Socrates illustrated the point using an image of ants and frogs around a pond, *Phd.* 109b (see 3.1). And see Purcell (2003).

currents frequently caused trouble for sailors.[2] In some cases, being driven adrift ended well and even resulted in geographical discoveries. When a ship from Samos captained by Colaeus tried to sail from the island of Platea off Libya (modern Bomba) to Egypt, for example, it was carried away by winds through the Pillars of Heracles to Tartessus (on the southern coast of Iberia) (Hdt. 4.152), while Q. Metellus Celer claimed that as a proconsul in Gaul (62 BCE) he was introduced to Indians who said they had drifted from Indian waters to the shores of Germany, proving that the sea was continuous (Nepos in Mela 3.45). But such adventures usually ended badly. Echoes of other frightening sites at sea were the legendary clashing rocks (Symplegades) at the Bosporus or near Sicily, and the monsters Scylla and Charybdis. This mix of reality and fantasy reflects the fact that navigators could not predict weather conditions or foresee undercurrents, making it safer to sail with the coast constantly in sight. In this way, it was also possible to disembark at night and to obtain supplies and equipment, although the procedure also made journeys significantly longer than a (theoretical) straight line between two points. Expeditions outside the Mediterranean also hugged the coast and were in fact generally circumnavigations. Sailing trips were limited to daytime and to the favourable season, usually May to October.[3] Besides these natural hindrances (topography, light and weather), pirates sometimes caused seafarers trouble as well.

Despite these obstacles, regular commercial routes as well as proactive exploration significantly widened the ancient world's maritime horizons. It is accordingly possible to assess the extent of knowledge of coastal horizons and maritime waters in antiquity. These included: (1) the entire perimeter of the Mediterranean, including its islands; (2) the entire perimeter of the Black Sea; (3) the west coast of Africa to the Niger Delta at the Gulf of Guinea; (4) lower Scandinavia, Iceland, Britain and Scotland; (5) the Caspian and some sections of the northern sea; and (6) the Ocean north of an imaginary line from Zanzibar in Africa to Cape Comorin (Kanyakumari) at the southernmost tip of India, including the two gulfs of the Red Sea and the Arabian-Persian Gulf.[4]

Practical daily use of *periploi* is implied in a short address to Menippus included in a Greek poem by Crinagoras of Mytilene:

---

[2] *Od.* 3.286–292; Hdt. 7.186; Diod. Sic. 13.64.6; Virg. *Aen.* 5.192–193. These conditions produced the proverb: 'When you double Malea, forget your home' (Strabo 8.6.20).

[3] Casson (1971), 270–273.

[4] No evidence for the circumnavigation of Arabia: Salles (1988).

I am looking for a guiding *periplous* that will lead me
around the Cycladic Islands as far as old Scheria.
Menippus, my friend, expert in all geography,
help me a bit by writing a scholarly tour.
                                        (Gow and Page (1968), 218)

The poet refers to a legendary island: Scheria, possibly Corcyra (Corfu),[5]
was the Homeric island of the Phaeacians (*Od.* 6.8). But the context puts
it 'around the Cycladic Islands', and even if Scheria is legendary, the use of
a *periplous* for a pre-planned journey, and the possibility of ordering one
in written form from a scholarly savant is still implied. In other words,
even if the theoretical geographical reality is deficient, the practical one
may not be.

Expeditions by sea preceded similar journeys by land, which were
lengthier and therefore time-consuming, dangerous and frightening. It was
therefore only relatively late that systematic records of land-routes emerged,
in the form of itineraries. In certain places and periods, a network of roads
was established. This system served the administrative functions of powers such as the Persian and Roman empires, and included posts at fixed
intervals, intended to help travellers. The Persian Royal Road, Herodotus
reports (5.52), featured stations (*stathmoi*) intended in the first instance for
the king's administrators, where stables or inns at known intervals provided both animals and humans with refreshment and rest. These stations
were situated one day's march (5 *parasangs*, 150 *stadia*, 28 kilometres) apart,
which allowed distances to be measured according to the number of stations on the road between two points. The well-known journey of the
Greek mercenaries recorded in Xenophon's *Anabasis* and, later, the records
of Alexander's journeys, indicate the actual use of these posts:

The length of the journey they had made from Ephesus in Ionia to the battlefield was 93 stages, 535 *parasangs*, or 1,650 *stadia*. And the distance from the
battlefield to Babylon was said to be 360 *stadia*. (Xen. *Anab.* 2.2.6)[6]

Systematic records of distances prefigured compiled lists of routes in the
form of *itineraria*.

In addition to written catalogues, whether *periploi* or *itineraria*, which
were accessible only to a limited number of people and were mainly
of assistance in planning journeys, other devices such as milestones

---

[5] Pocock (1957).
[6] This paragraph is generally regarded as an interpolation; but in the present context, this is
irrelevant.

(*milliaria*) were publicly displayed along roads to help travellers orientate themselves.[7] The Romans systematized this principle and erected stone posts at regular intervals on their roads, indicating the distance between points on a linear route. This made orientating oneself easier, as Polybius indicates:

> From Emporium to Narbo it is about six hundred *stadia*, and from Narbo to the passage of the Rhône about sixteen hundred, this part of the road having now been carefully measured by the Romans and marked with milestones at every eighth *stadion*. (3.39.8)

How were actual measurements taken to produce such written guides for travellers? Objective evaluation began with the older method of estimated time of travel, but more precise methods and results became standard.[8] The initial motivation to measure land emerged from the legal need to define private lots. According to Strabo, geometry (literally land measuring) began in Egypt: because the boundaries between private fields were constantly changing due to the annual inundation of the Nile, yearly redefinition of lots was necessary (Strabo 16.2.24; 17.1.3). In Roman times, the practice of measuring land became a profession often associated with the erection of military camps. An officer functioned as *finitor* (from *finis*, 'boundary'), *gromaticus* (from *groma*, 'sun-dial'), *mensor* ('measurer'), *agrimensor* ('measurer of land') or *decempedator* (after an instrument that counted feet).[9]

Distances were also calculated for actual travel routes, maritime or continental, but not for the sake of theoretical records. This meant that in most cases someone actually made the trek, which was measured in accordance with its specific topographic conditions and not as the crow flies. There was thus a fundamental difference between measuring shorter distances and longer ones (see 3.1).

Alexander of Macedon included in his entourage commissioned measurers or pacers (*bematistae*) such as Baiton, who documented his records in his *Stages (stathmoi) in Alexander's Journey* (Athen. 442 B). Even then, pacers were occupied with distances already travelled and not with the distances ahead of them. A later record of stages for the use of merchants was produced in the first century BCE by Isidorus of Charax, who composed his *Stathmoi Parthikoi*.[10] In it he provided a detailed list of sites

---

[7] Salway (2001); Laurence (2004).   [8] Lewis (2001), 19–22.
[9] Lewis (2001), esp. 120–139; Cuomo (2007), 107–113.
[10] Text: *GGM* 1.244–256; *FGrHist* 781; Schoff (1914).

along the caravan trail from Zeugma (in modern Turkey) to India, indicating distances in *schoeni*.[11]

One aspect of the systematization of recording distances was the establishment of fixed points of reference.[12] The gates of the Caspian Sea, at the crossroads near its southern exit, were the point of reference for roads and distances throughout the Persian Empire.[13] In 522 BCE, Peisistratus, the grandson of the homonymous Athenian tyrant, erected in the Athenian agora the Altar of the Twelve Gods, which was regarded as the centre of the Attic road network.[14] So too in the centre of Augustan Rome, and probably as part of the general geographical awareness of the age, a 'Golden Milestone' (*milliarium aureum*) was erected from which all roads in Italy nominally began, and all distances were measured relatively.[15] This monument symbolized the centrality of Rome. The stone itself has not survived (though its base has), but written evidence shows that names of major cities in the Empire and their distance from the city of Rome were engraved on it.

Inscriptions on larger stones, which functioned as monumental milestones, were found in north-western Europe and in Africa.[16] The monument in Tongres, Belgium, for instance, is a large octagonal block dated to *c.* 200 CE and inscribed with lists of sites and distances along several roads that met at the point where the stone was placed.[17]

A unique monument including geographical information related to travel was the *Stadiasmus Lyciae* dated to 43 CE and discovered in 1993.[18] Its reconstruction shows that it was erected in Patara by Q. Veranius, the governor of Lycia, and consisted of a rectangular stone 5.5 metres high, 1.6 metres wide and 2.35 metres deep, inscribed in Greek on three of its four sides. The front included a eulogy to the Emperor Claudius, dedicated by the Lycians. On top of this stone there was possibly a bronze equestrian statue of the emperor. The other two sides displayed a description of the province's road network, in the form of itineraries starting in Patara, listing provincial cities and using Greek *stadia*. Naturally, such a monument was publicly accessible, and it must have had meaning even for illiterate passers-by.

---

[11] *Schoeni* – originally an Egyptian unit of length adopted by the Greeks and measuring 40 *stadia*.
[12] Compare the fourth-century CE Byzantine *Million* monument in Constantinople and modern 'kilometre zero' points.
[13] Standish (1970).   [14] Thuc. 6.54.6; Hdt. 2.7.
[15] Plut. *Galba* 24.4; Brodersen (1996/97). For the so-called 'map' of Agrippa, see chapter 4.
[16] Brodersen (2001), 13–14; Salway (2001), 55–56.
[17] *CIL* XIII 9158.
[18] *SEG* 51 (2001), 1832; Isik *et al.* (2001); Sahin and Adak (2007).

Nautical distances were not calculated in the same way, particularly as open-sea voyages were rare. Because coastal journeys were the rule, distances were computed according to the distance along the coastline (i.e., according to continental distances). The author of the *Periplus of the Erythraean Sea* (2.3) offered distances in *stadia* for waters closer and better known to him, and in *dromoi* ('runs') for further waters. A *dromos* was the distance sailed from morning to night, that is during daylight.[19] Gradually, remote coasts outside the main frame of the *oikoumenê*, such as those in western Africa, the British Isles, northern Europe and Taprobane (Sri Lanka), were measured, and the size of the globe calculated. But the common notion still held that the Ocean was beyond reach, and therefore boundless and incalculable.[20]

Definition of the shape and calculation of the size of specific topographic features was essential for accurate geographical reports, but first and foremost for military purposes. A sea or land attack might succeed or fail depending on the commander's ability to assess the size of the region intended for passage or occupation. Basic assessments were crucial to a successful campaign: was a body of water a lake, a gulf, a sea or an ocean? Would crossing it require three hours, two days or two months? Seeking such information was also a function of the Greek taste for accuracy. How, then, were details of the size and shape of geographical features to be discovered and presented, for example, in the case of islands, mountains, plains and territorial sections with specific political identities?

The starting point for this process was the ability to grasp the entire body, i.e. to circumnavigate it (if an island) or to reach its limits (if a terrestrial region). Once a unit had been assigned mental limits, attempts were made to convey its size and – a more complicated task – its shape to an audience without any graphic aids. Size was measured along linear features defining the figure. These measurements were usually taken on a more or less flat surface and by simple procedures, mainly pacing or applying measuring rods and hodometers.

Practical needs, assisted by technical devices, thus stimulated the demand for accurate geographical records. At the same time, geographical documentation could support physical orientation in the field. This was one of the premises of Strabo in constructing his *Geography*, as a pragmatic composition offered, not only to scholars with an academic

---

[19] Casson (1989), 278–282. See also Vitruvius' application of the *hodometer* to distances at sea: *De arch.* 10.9.5–7.
[20] Heidel (1976); Romm (1992).

interest in geography, but also (and more importantly) to politicians and generals in need of information about foreign countries (Strabo 1.1.17). As emphasized above (chapter 4), we lack any physical remains of classical maps. Hints at such graphic representations (Strepsiades in Aristophanes, Aristagoras in Herodotus) do not yield much information about their nature. Nor is there any specific testimony about a general walking, sailing or riding about with an *itinerarium*, *periplous* or *periodos gês* in hand. It nonetheless seems reasonable to assume that some facts and ideas about foreign countries were available, and that men whose professions required frequent travel could find out in advance roughly where they were going.

5.2 POPULAR GEOGRAPHICAL KNOWLEDGE

In all likelihood, the Greek and Roman masses knew their immediate neighbourhood, their town or city, and possibly (depending on their origin, period and profession) some routes around their dwellings or even other towns and foreign countries. Apart from this daily physical experience, they probably had a vague knowledge of more remote places and foreign peoples. As we have seen, there were many different sorts of geographical texts, differing in genre, goal and content, but almost always addressed and available only to a limited section of the population: the literate and, in particular, intellectuals. Beside these channels of information, however, which form the core of classical geographical notions, there were others as well, which were available to a public wider than those who could read. Common people could *hear* particulars and *see* images of geographical information such as toponyms, foreign ethnic faces and dress, and extraordinary local details such as the pyramids in Egypt. Although fifth-century BCE Athens was different from Republican Rome in its politics, socio-economic conditions, mentality and scope of geographical knowledge, popular knowledge of geography must have been absorbed in similar ways throughout antiquity.

How much did the wider public know? What was their idea of the world? And to what extent could they mentally place exotic sites, nations and natural features? No definite answer can be given to these questions. Due to the lack of good evidence, it is also impossible to assess differences in degrees of geographical knowledge among various sections within the larger group of average individuals (men versus women; city dwellers versus residents of the countryside; citizens versus foreigners; and those in professions such as sailing, trading and positions of military command, which must have enhanced personal geographical experience). Hints of the extent of geographical awareness among the masses can, however, be gleaned from popular media.

Speeches addressed to the public were in some periods a central feature of political and administrative life. In democratic Athens, for instance, such speeches were addressed to all Athenian citizens, and the audience included men of varying economic and social status. Since speakers aspired to motivate the crowd to vote for a specific measure, they wanted to communicate clearly with their audience and to ensure that they understood what was being discussed. Some of the issues under discussion pertained directly to geographical data, for instance when military endeavours on specific battlefields were in question. Thucydides indicated the ignorance of ordinary Athenians about geographical conditions in Sicily (6.1.2), but Athenian orators often introduced toponyms into their speeches. Andocides, for instance, referred to Athenian aspirations to recover the islands of Lemnos, Scyros and Imbros (*On the Peace with Sparta*. 3.14). Did his listeners all know exactly what was at stake?

The audiences for tragedies and comedies in the theatre were more or less identical with the citizen body. Accordingly they included some illiterate individuals who could follow the performance and hear its contents, as well as more educated people. City-dwellers rather than common people from the countryside probably predominated. But all spectators could hear this:

> To earth's remotest limit we come
> To the Scythian land, an untrodden solitude.
> (Aeschylus (?), *Prometheus Bound*, 1–2)

They could then possibly identify the limits of the earth with the Scythians, even without having met a Scythian, and without being able to place the country mentally.

Referring to regions that were more 'domestic' for the Greeks, Aristophanes inserted the following expression: 'When the wolves and the white crows shall dwell together between Corinth and Sicyon' (*Birds*, 968). This meant 'never and nowhere', but to grasp the idea one had to know that Corinth and Sicyon bordered on one another, and thus that there is no space between the two regions.

A similar incorporation of geographical data features in Roman plays and speeches addressed to popular assemblies. But in all these cases it is difficult to assess the number of listeners or spectators, what they absorbed, what they remembered and how they understood what they heard and saw. All we can hope to estimate is the information available to the crowds, and how authors and artists might have wished to impress their audiences. At the same time, the assumption of an orator or a dramatist that his audience would respond to, or recognize, specific geographical details may have not represented reality, that is, the audience may not have followed the presenter. A speaker might also use unknown toponyms to confuse the audience, or to create an effect by playing on the fact that they *do not* know certain places. Finally, two people attending the same play or listening to the same speech would inevitably receive different impressions.

Despite these reservations, some general conclusions regarding geographical knowledge among the masses can be drawn, particularly if we add other channels of information, such as proverbial expressions. Proverbs by definition represent popular experience and wit. While speeches and plays reveal what people might know, or what geographical landmarks authors may have assumed a crowd would recognize, proverbs offer a chance to evaluate what common people knew and expressed in their everyday means of communication. Thus proverbial expressions may reflect first-hand experience acquired by ordinary people who travelled as sailors or soldiers, and who conveyed their impressions to family and friends back home. We cannot be sure that all, or even most, ordinary people could fully understand the place references within such proverbs, but even if they could not tell where exactly a certain *polis* or *ethnos* was located, they could at least gain some notion of features of places or of the atmosphere associated with them, and this seems to have enlarged their mental world. Three examples, Greek and Latin, demonstrate this.

The Greek expression 'You live in Keskos (*Keskon oikeis*)' [21] denoted an individual's lack of wit, because Keskos was a godforsaken place at the back of beyond in Pamphylia. Even for those unfamiliar with the exact location of the place, the proverb delivered some basic geographical information: there is a place named Keskos; Keskos is at the back of beyond. The Latin idiom *Tagus aurifer*, meaning 'gold-bearing Tagus', referred to a river in Spain (modern Tajo) famous for its gold.[22] And *Ultima Thule* denoted the extreme north. One does not have to be able to pick out these sites on a globe to absorb some geographical ideas about them and, needless to say, one does not have to have been there.

[21] Leutsch and Scheidewin (1965), 99.
[22] Otto (1962), 340, 348.

Finally, an important medium accessible to the public without any intellectual pre-requirements was visual artefacts and monuments. In a way, these were even more widely accessible than speeches and plays because they did not involve language. Examples of this category of evidence are the national portraits at Aphrodisias that show a series of foreign faces, or a bare-breasted, helmeted female warrior labelled 'Britannia' beneath the knee of a Roman soldier;[23] ethnic and geographical personifications on Roman triumphal monuments, such as Parthians on the cuirass of the Prima Porta Augustus or Dacians on Trajan's column; and scenes involving foreign prisoners on the Arch of Constantine;[24] and the so-called Nilotic mosaics offering images of foreign landscapes.[25] Even the monumental milestones mentioned above could have a 'geographical effect' on passengers, including the illiterate.

We now return to the questions asked at the beginning of this book: how could men discover that the earth was round? How did they estimate its size? How did traders and settlers search for and discover new land in unknown countries? And how did generals set out with armies from Greece through Asia Minor to Iran and India? It seems fair to say that Greeks and Romans in classical antiquity did all this impelled by a combination of necessity and curiosity. They did this by trial and error (there were unsuccessful military campaigns, and journeys of discovery that failed because of geographical ignorance), using technical, even if simple, solutions and tools; and by going on planned journeys and voyages of discovery. All these enabled these pre-modern societies to break new ground and to record their experience and thoughts in writing.

---

[23] Smith (1988).
[24] Holliday (1997); Beard (2009). Triumphal processions could also arouse 'geographical emotions' through foreign prisoners and booty.
[25] Versluys (2002).

Bibliography

Abulafia, D. (2011) *The Great Sea: A Human History of the Mediterranean*, Oxford.

Aczel, A.D. (2001) *The Riddle of the Compass: The Invention that Changed the World*, New York.

Aerts, W.J. (1994) 'Alexander the Great and ancient travel stories', in Z. von Martels (ed.), *Travel Fact and Travel Fiction: Studies on Fiction, Literary Tradition, Scholarly Discovery and Obsevation in Travel Writing*, Leiden: 30–38.

Albu, E. (2005) 'Imperial geography and the medieval Peutinger Map', *Imago Mundi* 57: 36–148.

Alzinger, W. (1977) 'Ein Stadtplanfund in Aguntum', *Antike Welt* 8 (2): 37–41.

Amato, E. (2005) *Dionisio di Alessandria: Descrizione della terra abitata*, Milan.

Arafat, K.W. (1996) *Pausanias' Greece. Ancient Artists and Roman Rulers*, Cambridge.

Armayor, O.K. (1978) 'Did Herodotus ever go to the Black Sea?', *HSPh* 82: 45–62.

(1980a) 'Did Herodotus ever go to Egypt?', *JARCE* 15: 59–73.

(1980b) 'Sesostris and Herodotus' autopsy of Thrace, Colchis, inland Asia Minor, and the Levant', *HSPh* 84: 51–74.

(1985) *Herodotus' Autopsy of the Fayoum: Lake Moeris and the Labyrinth of Egypt*, Amsterdam.

Arnaud, P. (1989) 'Une deuxième lecture de bouclier de Doura-Europos', *CRAI* 1989: 373–389.

Aujac, G. (1966) *Strabon et la science de son temps*, Paris.

(1975) *La géographie dans le monde antique*, Paris.

(1993) *Claude Ptolémée, astronome, astrologue, géographe: connaissance et représentation du monde habité*, Paris.

Austin, N.J.E. and Rankov, N.B. (1995) *Exploratio: Military and Political Intelligence in the Roman World from the Second Punic War to the Battle of Adrianople*, London.

Bacon, J.R. (1931) 'The geography of the Orphic *Argonautica*', *CQ* 25 (3/4): 172–183.

Ball, J. (1942) *Egypt in the Classical Geographers*, Cairo.

Ballabriga, A. (1986) *Le soleil et le tartare: L'image mythique du monde en Grèce archaïque*, Paris.

(1998) *Les fictions d'Homère: L'invention mythologique et cosmographique dans l'Odysée*, Paris.

Barber, G.L. (1979) *The Historian Ephorus*, New York (repr. of 1935 edn.).

Baslez, M.F. (1995) 'Fleuves et voies d'eau dans l'*Anabase*', in P. Briant (ed.), *Dans les pas des Dix Mille: Peuples et pays du Proche-Orient vus par un grec*, Toulouse: 79–88.

Batty, R. (2000) 'Mela's Phoenician geography', *JRS* 90: 70–94.

Baynham, E. (2001) 'Alexander and the Amazons', *CQ* 51 (1): 115–126.

Beagon, M. (1992) *Roman Nature: The Thought of Pliny the Elder*, Oxford.

Beard, M. (2006) 'The artists of antiquity', *Times Literary Supplement*, 8 March 2006, 1–3.

(2009) *The Roman Triumph*, Cambridge, MA.

Bennet, J. (1999) 'The Mycenaean conceptualization of space or Pylian geography (… yet again!)', in S. Deger-Jalkotzy, S. Hiller and O. Panagl (eds.), *Floreant studia mycenaea*, vol. 1, Vienna: 131–157.

Berger, H. (1880) *Die geographische Fragmente des Eratosthenes*, Leipzig.

Berggren, J.L. and Jones, A. (2000) *Ptolemy's* Geography. *An Annotated Translation of the Theoretical Chapters*, Princeton, NJ, and Oxford.

Bertrand, A.C. (1997) 'Stumbling through Gaul: Maps, intelligence and Caesar's *Bellum Gallicum*', *AHB* 11: 107–122.

Bertrand, J.-M. (1989) 'De l'emploi des métaphores descriptives par les géographes de l'antiquité', *DHA* 15 (1): 63–73.

Bickerman, E.J. (1952) 'Origines gentium', *CPh* 47 (2): 65–68.

Biraschi, A.M. (2005) 'Strabo and Homer: A chapter in cultural history', in D. Dueck, H. Lindsay and S. Pothecary (eds.), *Strabo's Cultural Geography: The Making of a* Kolossourgia, Cambridge: 73–85.

Bloch, R.S. (2000) 'Geography without territory: Tacitus' digression on the Jews and its ethnographic context', in J.U. Kalms (ed.), *Internationales Josephus Kolloquium, Aarhus 1999*, Münster: 38–54.

Blok, J.H. (1995) *The Early Amazons. Modern and Ancient Perspectives on a Persistent Myth*, Leiden.

Boardman, J. (1999) *The Greeks Overseas*, London and New York, 4th edn.

Bolton, J.D.P. (1962) *Aristeas of Proconnesus*, Oxford.

Bonnafé, A. (2000) 'Le lieu scénique, "carte" du "territoire" de la pièce: le mode d'emploi athénien dans les tragédies', in A. Bonnafé, J.C. Decourt and B. Helly (eds.), *L'espace et ses représentations*, Lyon: 73–82.

Bosworth, A.B. (1996) 'The historical setting of Megasthenes' *Indica*', *CPh* 91 (2): 113–127.

Bowen, A.C. and Todd, R.B. (2004) *Cleomedes' Lectures on Astronomy*, Berkeley, CA.

Bowersock, G.W. (1983) *Roman Arabia*, Cambridge, MA.

Bowie, E. (2004) 'Dénys d'Alexandrie. Un poète grec dans l'empire romain', *REA* 106: 177–186.

Bowman, G. (1998) 'Mapping history's redemption: Eschatology and topography in the *Itinerarium Burdigalense*', in L.I. Levine (ed.), *Jerusalem: Its Sanctity and Centrality to Judaism, Christianity and Islam*, New York and Jerusalem: 163–187.

Braund, D. (1996) 'River frontiers in the environmental psychology of the Roman world', in D.L. Kennedy (ed.), *The Roman Army in the East*, Ann Arbor, MI: 43–47.

Brein, F. (1980) 'Das Aguntiner Kuckucksei', *Römisches Österreich* 8: 5–26.

Brodersen, K. (1994a) *Dionysios von Alexandria, Das Lied von der Welt*, Hildesheim, Zürich, New York.

   (1994b) *Pomponius Mela, Kreuzfahrt durch die Alte Welt. Zweisprachige Ausgabe*, Darmstadt.

   (1996/97) '*Miliarium Aureum* und *Umbilicus Romae*: Zwei Mittelpunkte des römischen Reiches?', *Würzburger Jahrbücher* 21: 273–283.

   (2001) 'The presentation of geographical knowledge for travel and transport in the Roman world: *Itineraria non tantum adnotata sed etiam picta*', in C. Adams and R. Laurence (eds.), *Travel and Geography in the Roman Empire*, London and New York: 7–21.

   (2003) *Terra Cognita: Studien zur römischen Raumerfassung*, Hildesheim and New York, 2nd edn.

   (2010) 'Space and geography', in A. Barchiesi and W, Scheidel (eds.), *Handbook of Roman Studies*, Oxford: 827–837.

   (2011) 'Mapping Pliny's world: The achievement of Solinus', *BICS* 54 (1): 63–88.

Brodersen, K. and Elsner, J. (eds.) (2009) *Images and Texts on the 'Artemidorus Papyrus'* (*Historia Einzelschriften* 124), Stuttgart.

Brown, T.S. (1949) *Onesicritus. A Study in Hellenistic Historiography*, Berkeley and Los Angeles.

   (1955) 'The reliability of Megasthenes', *AJPh* 76 (1): 18–33.

   (1957) 'The merits and weaknesses of Megasthenes', *Phoenix* 11 (1): 12–24.

   (1988) 'Herodotus' travels', *AncW* 17: 67–75.

Brunt, P.A. (1978) 'Laus imperii', in P.D.A. Garnsey and C.R. Whittaker (eds.), *Imperialism in the Ancient World*, Cambridge: 159–191.

Bulling, A.G. (1978) 'Ancient Chinese maps: Two naps discovered in a Han Dynasty tomb from the second century BC', *Expedition* 20 (2): 16–25.

Bunbury, E.H. (1883) *A History of Ancient Geography*, New York, 2nd edn.

Burian, J. (2007) 'Periplous', in *Brill's New Pauly*, Leiden: 799–801.

Burns, T.S. (2003) *Rome and the Barbarians: 100 BC–AD 400*, Baltimore.

Burr, V. (1932) *Nostrum Mare: Ursprung und Geschichte der Namen des Mittelmeers und seine Teilmeere im Altertum*, Stuttgart.

Burstein, S.M. (1989) *Agatharchides of Cnidus*, On the Erythraean Sea, London.

Cajori, F. (1929) 'History of determinations of the heights of mountains', *Isis* 12 (3): 482–514.

Campbell, B. (1996) 'Shaping the rural environment: Surveyors in ancient Rome', *JRS* 86: 74–99.

   (2000) *The Works of the Roman Land Surveyors* (*JRS* Monograph no. 9), London (repr. 2008).

Canfora, L. (2007) *The True History of the So-called Artemidorus Papyrus*, Bari.

Cappelletto, P. (2003) *I frammenti di Mnasea: Introduzione, testo e commento*, Milan.

Carpenter, R. (1956) 'A trans-Saharan caravan route in Herodotus', *AJA* 60 (3): 231–242.

Cartledge, P. (1993) *The Greeks: A Portrait of Self and Others*, Oxford.

(2001) 'Greeks and "barbarians"', in A.F. Christidis (ed.), *A History of Ancient Greece from the Beginnings to Late Antiquity*, Cambridge: 307–313.

Cary, M. (1949) *The Geographic Background of Greek and Roman History*, Oxford.

Cary, M. and Warmington, E.H. (1963) *The Ancient Explorers*, Harmondsworth.

Caspari, M.O.B. (1910) 'On the *Ges Periodos* of Hecataeus', *JHS* 30: 236–248.

Casson, L. (1971) *Ships and Seamanship in the Ancient World*, Princeton, NJ.

(1974) *Travel in the Ancient World*, Toronto.

(1989) *The* Periplus Maris Erythraei, Princeton, NJ.

(1994) *Ships and Seafaring in Ancient Times*, London.

Chaumont, M.L. (1984) 'Études d'histoire parthe v. La route royale des Parthes de Zeugma à Séleucie du Tigre d'après l'itinéraire d'Isidore de Charax', *Syria* 61: 63–107.

Clarke, K. (1999) *Between Geography and History: Hellenistic Constructions of the Roman World*, Oxford.

Clay, D. (1992) 'The World of Hesiod', *Ramus* 21: 131–55.

Coleman, J. (ed.) (1997) *Greeks and Barbarians: Essays on the Interactions between Greeks and Non-Greeks in Antiquity and the Consequences for Eurocentrism*, Bethesda, MD.

Constantakopoulou, C. (2007) *The Dance of the Islands: Insularity, Networks, the Athenian Empire and the Aegean World*, Oxford.

Conticello de' Spagnolis, M. (1984) *Il tempio dei Dioscuri nel Circo Flaminio*, Rome.

Cordano, F. (1992) *La geografia degli antichi*, Bari.

Cosgrove, D. (2008) *Geography and Vision: Seeing, Imagining and Representing the World*, New York.

Courtney, E. (ed.) (1993) *The Fragmentary Latin Poets*, Oxford.

Crone, P. (1989) *Pre-Industrial Societies: Anatomy of the Pre-Modern World*, Oxford.

Cumont, F. (1926) *Fouilles de Doura-Europos (1922–1923)*, vols. i–ii, Paris.

Cunliffe, B.W. (1988) *Greeks, Romans and Barbarians: Spheres of Interaction*, London.

(2003) *The Extraordinary Voyage of Pytheas the Greek*, New York.

Cuomo, S. (2007) *Technology and Culture in Greek and Roman Antiquity*, Cambridge.

Davies, H.E.H. (1998) 'Designing Roman roads', *Britannia* 29: 1–16.

Delage, E. (1930) *La géographie dans les* Argonautiques *d'Apollonios de Rhodes*, Paris.

Dench, E. (2007) 'History and ethnography', in J. Marincola (ed.), *A Companion to Greek and Roman Historiography*, vol. 2, Malden, MA: 493–503.

Desanges, J. (1964) 'Note sur la datation de l'expédition de Julius Maternus au pays d'Aysymba', *REL* 23 (4): 713–725.

Detlefsen, D. (1972) *Die Anordnung der geographischen Bücher des Plinius und Ihre Quellen*, Rome.

Dickie, M.W. (1995) 'The geography of Homer's world', in Ø. Andersen and M.W. Dickie (eds.), *Homer's World: Fiction, Tradition, Reality*, Athens: 29–56.

Dicks, D.R. (1960) *The Geographical Fragments of Hipparchus*. London.

Dilke, O.A.W. (1985) *Greek and Roman Maps*, Baltimore.

    (1987) 'Maps in the service of the state', in J.B. Harley and D. Woodward (eds.), *The History of Cartography*, vol. 1: *Cartography in Prehistoric, Ancient and Medieval Europe and the Mediterranean*, Chicago: 201–211.

    (1988) 'Table ronde on Graeco-Roman cartography (Paris 1987)', *JRA* 1: 89–94.

Diller, A. (1934) 'Geographical latitudes in Eratosthenes, Hipparchus and Posidonius', *Klio* 27: 258–269.

    (1949) 'The ancient measurements of the Earth', *Isis* 40 (1): 6–9.

    (1952) *The Tradition of the Minor Greek Geographers*, New York.

    (1955) 'The authors named Pausanias', *TAPhA* 86: 268–279.

    (1975) 'Agathemerus' *Sketch of Geography*', *GRBS* 16: 59–76.

Dillery, J. (1998) 'Hecataeus of Abdera: Hyperboreans, Egypt and the *Interpretatio Graeca*', *Historia* 47 (3): 255–275.

Dion, R. (1977) *Aspects politiques de la géographie antique*, Paris.

Drews, R. (1963) 'Ephorus and history written κατὰ γένος', *AJPh* 84 (3): 244–255.

Dueck, D. (2000) *Strabo of Amasia: A Greek Man of Letters in Augustan Rome*, London.

    (2003) 'The Augustan concept of "An empire without limits"', *Göttinger Beiträge zur Asienforschung* 2–3: 211–228.

    (2005a) 'Strabo's use of poetry', in D. Dueck, H. Lindsay and S. Pothecary (eds.), *Strabo's Cultural Geography: The Making of a* Kolossourgia, Cambridge: 86–107.

    (2005b) 'The parallelogram and the pinecone: Definition of geographical shapes in Greek and Roman geography on the evidence of Strabo', *AncSoc* 35: 19–57.

Edelstein, L. and Kidd, I.G. (eds.) (1972) *Posidonius, The Fragments*, Cambridge.

Ellis, L. and Kidner, F.L. (eds.) (2004) *Travel, Communication and Geography in Late Antiquity: Sacred and Profane*, Burlington, VT.

Elsner, J. (2001) 'Structuring "Greece": Pausanias's *Periegesis* as a literary construct', in S.E. Alcock, J.F. Cherry and J. Elsner (eds.), *Pausanias. Travel and Memory in Ancient Greece*, Oxford: 3–20.

Elton, H. (2004) 'Cilicia, geography, and the late Roman Empire', in L. Ellis and F.L. Kidner (eds.), *Travel, Communication and Geography in Late Antiquity: Sacred and Profane*, Burlington, VT: 5–11.

Engels, D. (1985) 'The length of Eratosthenes' stade', *AJPh* 106 (3): 298–311.

Engels, J. (2007) 'Geography and history', in J. Marincola (ed.), *A Companion to Greek and Roman Historiography*, vol. 2, Malden, MA: 541–552.

Evans, J. (1998) *The History and Practice of Ancient Astronomy*, Oxford.

Evans, R. (1999) 'Ethnography's freak show: The grotesques at the edges of the Roman earth', *Ramus* 28 (1): 54–73.

(2005) 'Geography without people: Mapping in Pliny *Historia Naturalis* books 3–6', *Ramus* 34 (1): 47–74.

Feldherr, A. (1999) 'Putting Dido on the map: Genre and geography in Vergil's underworld', *Arethusa* 32: 85–122.

Finkelberg, M. (1998) 'The geography of the *Prometheus Vinctus*', *RhM* 141 (2): 119–141.

Fortenbaugh, W. and Schütrumpf, E. (eds.) (2001) *Dicaearchus of Messana: Text, Translation and Discussion*, New Brunswick, NJ.

Fraser, P.M. (1972) 'Geographical writing', in *Ptolemaic Alexandria*, vol. 1, Oxford: 520–553.

Funke, P. and Haake, M. (2006) 'Theaters of war: Thucydidean topography', in A. Rengakos and A. Tsakmakis (eds.), *Brill's Companion to Thucydides*, Leiden: 369–384.

Futo Kennedy, R. (2006) 'Justice, geography and empire in Aeschylus' *Eumenides*', *ClAnt* 25 (1): 35–72.

Gallazzi, C., Kramer, B. and Settis, S. (eds.) (2008) *Il papiro di Artemidoro*, vols. 1–2, Milan.

Geiger, J. (1985) *Cornelius Nepos and Ancient Political Biography*, Stuttgart.

Geus, K. (2002) *Eratosthenes von Kyrene: Studien zur hellenistischen Kultur- und Wissenschaftsgeschichte*, Munich.

(2003) 'Space and geography', in A. Erskine (ed.), *A Companion to the Hellenistic World,* Malden, MA: 232–245.

(2004) 'Measuring the Earth and the *Oikoumene*: Zones, meridians, *sphragides* and some other geographical terms used by Eratosthenes of Kyrene', in R. Talbert and K. Brodersen (eds.), *Space in the Roman World: Its Perception and Presentation*, Münster: 11–26.

Geyer, P., Cunz, O., Franceschini, A. *et al.* (eds.) (1965) *Itineraria et Alia Geographica*, Turnhout.

Giannini, A. (1966) *Paradoxographorum Graecorum Reliquiae*, Milan.

Gomarasca, M.A. (2009) *Basics of Geomatics*, Dordrecht, Heidelberg, London and New York.

Gould, J. (1989) *Herodotus*, London.

Gow, A.S.F. and Page, D.L. (eds.) (1968) *The Greek Anthology: The Garland of Philip and Some Contemporary Epigrams*, vol. 1, Cambridge.

Grant, M. (2000) 'Seneca's tragic geography', *Latomus* 59 (1): 88–95.

Green, C.M.C. (1993) '*De Africa et eius incolis*: The function of geography and ethnography in Sallust's history of the Jugurthine War', *AncW* 24: 185–197.

Grilli, A. (1989) 'La geografía di Agrippa', in *Il bimillenario di Agrippa*, Genoa: 127–146.

Grosjean, G. (1977) *Der katalanische Weltatlas vom Jahre 1375*, Dietikon–Zurich.

Habicht, C. (1985) *Pausanias' Guide to Ancient Greece*, Berkeley, Los Angeles and London.

Hall, E.M. (1987) 'The geography of Euripides' *Iphigeneia among the Taurians*', *AJPh* 108: 427–433.

(1989) *Inventing the Barbarian: Greek Self-definition through Tragedy*, Oxford.

Harder, M.A. (1994) 'Travel descriptions in the *Argonautica* of Apollonius Rhodius' in Z. von Martels (ed.), *Travel Fact and Travel Fiction: Studies on Fiction, Literary Tradition, Scholarly Discovery and Obsevation in Travel Writing*, Leiden: 16–29.

Harder, M.A., Regtuit, R.F. and Wakker, G.C. (eds.) (2009) *Nature and Science in Hellenistic Poetry*, Groningen.

Hardie, P.R. (1985) 'Imago Mundi: Cosmological and ideological aspects of the shield of Achilles', *JHS* 105: 11–31.

(1986) *Virgil's* Aeneid: *Cosmos and Imperium*, Oxford.

(ed.) (2009) *Paradox and the Marvellous in Augustan Literature and Culture*, Oxford.

Hardwick, L. (1990) 'Ancient Amazons: Heroes, outsiders or women?', *G & R* 37 (1): 14–36.

Harrison, T. (ed.) (2002) *Greeks and Barbarians*, Edinburgh.

Hartog, F. (1988) *The Mirror of Herodotus: The Representation of the Other in the Writing of History*, Berkeley and Los Angeles.

Harvey, P.D.A. (1991) *Medieval Maps*, London.

Haselberger, L. (1994) 'Antike Bauzeichnung des Pantheon entdeckt', *Antike Welt* 25: 323–339.

(forthcoming) *Designing Graeco-Roman Architecture. From Didyma to the Pantheon.*

Healy, J.F. (1999) *Pliny the Elder on Science and Technology*, Oxford.

Heidel, W.A. (1976) *The Frame of the Ancient Greek Maps, with a Discussion of the Discovery of the Sphericity of the Earth*, New York.

Heisel, J.P. (1993) *Antike Bauzeichnungen*, Darmstadt.

Hill, J.E. (2009) *Through the Jade Gate to Rome: A Study of the Silk Routes during the Later Han Dynasty, 1st to 2nd Centuries CE*, Charleston, SC.

Holder, A. (1965) *Rufi Festi Avieni Carmina*, Hildesheim.

Holliday, P.J. (1997) 'Roman triumphal painting: Its function, development, and reception', *Art Bulletin* 79: 130–147.

Hope Simpson, R. and Lazenby, J.F. (1970) *The Catalogue of the Ships in Homer's* Iliad, Oxford.

Horden, P. and Purcell, N. (2000) *The Corrupting Sea: A Study of Mediterranean History*, Oxford and Malden, MA.

Hsu, M.-L. (1978) 'The Han maps and early Chinese cartography', *Annals of the Association of American Geographers* 68: 45–60.

(1984) 'Early Chinese cartography: Its mathematical and surveying backgrounds', in *Technical Papers of the 44th Meeting of the American Congress on Surveying and Mapping (1984)*, Washington, DC: 128–138.

Hunter, R. (2004) 'The *Periegesis* of Dionysius and the traditions of Hellenistic poetry', *REA* 106: 217–232.

Hutton, W. (2005) *Describing Greece: Landscape and Literature in the* Periegesis *of Pausanias*, Cambridge.

Hyde, W.W. (1947) *Ancient Greek Mariners*, New York.

Isaac, B. (1992) *The Limits of Empire: The Roman Army in the East*, Oxford.

(1996) 'Eusebius and the geography of the Roman provinces', in D.L. Kennedy (ed.), *The Roman Army in the East*, Ann Arbor, MI: 153–167.

(2004) *The Invention of Racism in Classical Antiquity*, Princeton, NJ, and Oxford.

Isik, F., Iskan, H. and Cevik, N. (2001) *Miliarium Lyciae: Das Wegweisermonument von Patara*, Antalya.

Jacob, C. (1983) 'De l'art de compiler à la fabrication du merveilleux: Sur la para-doxographie grecque', *Lalies* 2: 121–140.

(1990) *La description de la terre habitée de Denys d'Alexandrie ou la leçon de géographie*, Paris.

(1991) *Géographie et ethnographie en Grèce ancienne*. Paris.

Janni, P. (1984) *La mappa e il periplo: Cartografia antica e spazio odologico*, Rome.

Johnston, A.E.M. (1967) 'The earliest preserved Greek map', *JHS* 87: 265–284.

Kajanto, I. (1965) *The Latin* Cognomina, Helsinki.

Keyser, P.T. (2001) 'The geographical work of Dikaiarchos', in W.W. Fortenbaugh and E. Schütrumpf (eds.), *Dicaearchus of Messana: Text, Translation and Discussion*, New Brunswick, NJ: 353–372.

Kiessling, E. (1914) 'Rhipaia ore', in *RE* I A 1: 846–916.

Klotz, A. (1931) 'Die geographischen "commentarii" des Agrippa und ihre Überreste', *Klio* 24: 38–58, 386–466.

Kolb, A. (2001) 'Transport and communication in the Roman state: the *cursus publicus*', in C. Adams and R. Laurence (eds.), *Travel and Geography in the Roman Empire*, London and New York: 95–105.

Korenjak, M. (2003) *Die Welt-Rundreise eines anonymen griechischen Autors ('Pseudo-Skymnos')*, Hildesheim.

Krebs, C.B. (2006) '"Imaginary geography" in Caesar's *Bellum Gallicum*', *AJPh* 127 (1): 111–136.

Krevans, N. (1983) 'Geography and the literary tradition in Theocritus 7', *TAPhA* 113: 201–220.

Kubtischek, W. (1919) 'Karten', in *RE* x 2: 2022–2149.

Laurence, R. (2004) 'Milestones, communications, and political stability', in L. Ellis and F.L. Kidner (eds.), *Travel, Communication and Geography in Late Antiquity: Sacred and Profane*, Burlington, VT: 41–57.

Lenfant, D. (2004) *Ctésias de Cnide: La Perse, l'Inde, autres fragments*, Paris.

(2011) *Le Perses vus par les Grecs: Lire les sources classiques sur l'empire achémé-nide*, Paris.

Leslie, D.D. and Gardiner, K.H.J. (1996) *The Roman Empire in Chinese Sources*, Rome.

Leutsch, E.L. and Scheidewin, F.G. (eds.) (1965) *Corpus Paroemiographorum Graecorum*, Hildesheim (repr. of 1839 edn.).

Levi, M.A. (1987) *Il mondo dei Greci e dei Romani*, Padua.

Lewis, M.J.T. (2001) *Surveying Instruments of Greece and Rome*, Cambridge.

Lipinski, E. (2004) *Itineraria Phoenicia*, Leuven.

Lisler, R.P. (1980) *The Travels of Herodotus*, London.

Lloyd, A.B. (1977) 'Necho and the Red Sea: Some considerations', *JEA* 63: 142–155.

Lozovsky, N. (2000) *The Earth Is Our Book: Geographical Knowledge in the Latin West ca. 400–1000*, Ann Arbor, MI.

McGroarty, K. (2006) 'Did Alexander the Great read Xenophon?', *Hermathena* 181: 105–124.

Majumdar, R.C. (1958) 'The *Indika* of Megasthenes', *JAOS* 78: 273–276.

Malkin, I. (ed.) (2001) *Ancient Perceptions of Greek Ethnicity*, Washington, DC.

Manfredi, V. (1986) *La strada dei Diecimila: Topografia e geografia dell'oriente di Senofonte*, Milan.

Marcotte, D. (1990) *Le poème géographique de Dionysios fils de Calliphon*, Louvain.

(2002) *Les géographes grecs: Pseudo-Scymnus*, Circuit de la terre, Paris.

Marenghi, G. (1958) *Arriano* Periplo del Ponte Eusino, Naples.

Marrou, H.I. (1965) *Histoire de l'éducation dans l'antiquité*, Paris, 6th edn.

Matthews, J.F. (2006) *The Journey of Theophanes: Travel, Business and Daily Life in the Roman East*, New Haven, CT.

Mauny, R. (2002) 'Trans-Saharan contacts and the Iron Age in West Africa', in *The Cambridge History of Africa*, vol. 1, Cambridge: 277–286.

Mayer, R. (1986) 'Geography and Roman poets', *G&R* 33 (1): 47–54.

Merrills, A. (2005) *History and Geography in Late Antiquity*, Cambridge.

Meyer, D. (2008) 'Apollonius as a Hellenistic geographer', in T.D. Papanghelis and A. Rengakos (eds.), *Brill's Companion to Apollonius Rhodius*, Leiden: 267–285.

Meyer, H.D. (1961) *Die Aussenpolitik des Augustus und die augusteiche Dichtung*, Cologne.

Michel, D. (1967) *Alexander als Vorbild für Pompeius, Caesar und Marcus Antonius*, Brussels.

Miller, K. (1895) *Mappaemundi II: Die kleineren Weltkarten*, Stuttgart.

(1898) *Mappaemundi VI: Rekonstruierte Karten*, Stuttgart.

Momigliano, A. (1975) *Alien Wisdom: The Limits of Hellenization*, Cambridge.

Mommsen, T. (1908) *Historische Schriften ii (= Gesammelte Schriften v)*, Berlin.

Montiglio, S. (2000) 'Wandering philosophers in Classical Greece', *JHS* 120: 86–105.

(2006) 'Should the aspiring wise man travel? A conflict in Seneca's thought', *AJPh* 127 (4): 553–586.

Morgan, T. (1998) *Literate Education in the Hellenistic and Roman World*, Cambridge.

Müllenhoff, K. (1875) 'Über die römische Weltkarte', *Hermes* 9: 182–195 (also in idem (1892) *Deutsche Altertumskunde*, vol. 3, Berlin: 298–311).

Müller, C. (1855–1861) *Geographici Graeci Minores*, Paris.

Murphy, T.M. (2004) *Pliny the Elder's* Natural History: *The Empire in the Encyclopedia*, Oxford.

Nakassis, D. (2004) 'Gemination at the horizons: East and west in the mythical geography of Archaic Greek epic', *TAPhA* 134 (2): 215–233.

Nicastro, N. (2008) *Circumference: Eratosthenes and the Ancient Quest to Measure the Globe*, New York.

Nicolet, C. (1991) *Space, Geography and Politics in the Early Roman Empire*, Ann Arbor, MI.

Nishimura-Jensen, J. (2000) 'The moving landscape in Apollonius' *Argonautica* and Callimachus' *Hymn to Delos*', *TAPhA* 130: 287–317.

Östenberg, I. (2009) *Staging the World. Spoils, Captives and Representations in the Roman Triumphal Procession*, Oxford.

Otto, A. (1962) *Die Sprichwörter und sprichwörtlichen Redensarten der Römer*, Hildesheim (originally published 1890).

Panchenko, D.V. (1997) 'Anaxagoras' argument against the sphericity of the earth', *Hyperboreus* 3 (1): 175–178.

(1998) 'Scylax' circumnavigation of India and its interpretation in early Greek geography, ethnography and cosmography, I', *Hyperboreus* 4 (2): 211–242.

(2003) 'Scylax' circumnavigation of India and its interpretation in early Greek geography, ethnography and cosmography, II', *Hyperboreus* 9 (2): 274–294.

Partsch, J. (1907) Review of Detlefsen (1907), *Wochenschrift für Klassische Philologie* 24: 1053–1062.

Pearson, L. (1938) 'Apollonius of Rhodes and the old geographers', *AJPh* 59: 443–459.

(1939) 'Thucydides and the geographical tradition', *CQ* 33: 49–54.

(1983) *The Lost Histories of Alexander the Great*, New York (originally published 1960).

Pédech, P. (1956) 'La géographie de Polybe: Structure et contenu du livre xxxiv des *Histoires*', *LEC* 24: 3–24.

(1974) 'L'analyse géographique chez Posidonius', in R. Chevallier (ed.), *Littérature gréco-romaine et géographie historique*, Paris: 31–43.

(1976) *La géographie des grecs*, Paris.

Philipp, H. (1936) 'Die Namen der Erdteile Europa, Asien und Afrika', *Petermanns Geographische Mitteilungen*, 109–110.

Philippi, F. (1880) *Zur Reconstruction der Weltkarte des Agrippa*, Marburg.

Picard, G.C. (1982) 'Le *Périple* d'Hannon', in H.G. Niemeyer (ed.), *Phönizier im westen*, Mainz: 175–180.

Piganiol, A. (1962) *Les documents cadastraux de la colonie romaine d'Orange*, Paris.

Piot, M. (2000) 'Le Rhône et l'Éridane dans les *Argonautiques*, ou les aventures de la géographie et de la légende', in A. Bonnafé, J.C. Decourt and B. Helly (eds.), *L'espace et ses représentations*, Lyon: 133–141.

Pocock, L.G. (1957) 'Samuel Butler and the site of Scheria', *G&R* 4 (2): 125–130.

Polignac, F. de (1995) *Cults, Territory, and the Origins of the Greek City-State*, Chicago and London, 2nd edn. (originally published in French 1984).

Pothecary, S. (1995) 'Strabo, Polybios, and the stade', *Phoenix* 49 (1): 49–67.

Pothou, V. (2009) *La place et le rôle de la digression dans l'oeuvre de Thucydide*, Stuttgart.

Pretzler, M. (2004) 'Turning travel into text: Pausanias at work', *G&R* 51 (2): 199–216.

(2005) 'Comparing Strabo with Pausanias: Greece in context vs. Greece in depth', in D. Dueck, H. Lindsay and S. Pothecary (eds.), *Strabo's Cultural Geography: The Making of a* Kolossourgia, Cambridge: 144–160.

(2007) *Pausanias: Travel Writing in Ancient Greece*, London.

Prontera, F. (ed.) (1983) *Geografia e geografi nel mondo antico: guida storica e critica*, Bari.

(1984) 'Prima di Strabone: Materiali per uno studio della geografia antica come genere letterario', in *Strabone. Contributi allo studio della personalità e dell'opera*, Perugia: 189–256.

(1992) '*Periploi*: sulla tradizione della geografia nautica presso i Greci', in *L'uomo e il mare nella civiltà occidentale: Da Ulisse a Cristoforo Colombo*, Genoa: 27–44.

Purcell, N. (2003) 'On the boundless sea of unlikeness? On defining the Mediterranean', *Mediterranean Historical Review* 18 (2) 9–29.

Purves, A.C. (2010) *Space and Time in Ancient Greek Narrative*, New York.

Raaflaub, K.A. and Talbert, R.J.A. (eds.) (2010) *Geography and Ethnography: Perceptions of the World in Pre-Modern Societies*, Chichester.

Rawson, E. (1985) 'Geography and ethnography', in E. Rawson, *Intellectual Life in the Late Roman Republic*, London: 250–266.

Rescher, N. (2005) *Cosmos and Logos: Studies in Greek Philosophy*, Frankfurt.

Riese, A. (1878) *Geographi Latini Minores*, Heilbronn.

Riley, M.T. (1995) 'Ptolemy's use of his predecessors' data', *TAPhA* 125: 221–250.

Ritschl, F. (1877) *Kleine philologische Schriften*, vol. 3, Leipzig.

Roller, D.W. (2003) *The World of Juba II and Kleopatra Selene: Royal Scholarship on Rome's African Frontier*, London.

(2004) *Scholarly Kings: The Fragments of Juba II of Mauretania, Archelaos of Kappadokia, Herod the Great and the Emperor Claudius*, Chicago.

(2006) *Through the Pillars of Herakles: Greco-Roman Exploration of the Atlantic*, New York and London.

(2010) *Eratosthenes' Geography: Fragments Collected and Translated, with Commentary and Additional Material*, Princeton, NJ.

Romer, F. (1998) *Pomponius Mela's Description of the World*, Ann Arbor, MI.

Romm, J.S. (1989a) 'Herodotus and mythic geography: The case of the Hyperboreans', *TAPhA* 119: 97–113.

(1989b) 'Aristotle's elephant and the myth of Alexander's scientific patronage', *AJPh* 110: 566–575.

(1992) *The Edges of the Earth in Ancient Thought: Geography, Exploration and Fiction*, Princeton, NJ.

(1998) *Herodotus*, New Haven, CT.

(2006) 'Herodotus and the natural world', in C. Dewald and J. Marincola (eds.), *The Cambridge Companion to Herodotus*, Cambridge: 178–191.

(2010) 'Continents, climates, and cultures: Greek theories of global structure', in K.A. Raaflaub and R.J.A. Talbert (eds.), *Geography and Ethnography: Perceptions of the World in Pre-Modern Societies*, Chichester: 215–235.

Rood, T. (2006) 'Herodotus and foreign lands', in C. Dewald and J. Marincola (eds.), *The Cambridge Companion to Herodotus*, Cambridge: 290–305.

Roseman, C.H. (1994) *Pytheas of Massalia*, On the Ocean, Chicago.

Rougé, J. (1988) 'La navigation en mer Érythrée dans l'antiquité', in J.F. Salles (ed.), *L'Arabie et ses mers bordières. i – Itinéraires et voisinages*, Lyon: 59–74.

Sáez Fernández, P. (1990) 'Estudio sobre una inscripción catastral colindante con Lacimurga', *Habis* 21: 205–227.

Sahin, S. and Adak, M. (2007) *Stadiasmus Patarensis: Itinera Romana Provinciae Lyciae*, Istanbul.

Salles, J.F. (1988) 'La circumnavigation de l'Arabie dans l'Antiquité classique', in J.F. Salles (ed.), *L'Arabie et ses mers bordières. i – Itinéraires et voisinages*, Lyon: 75–102.

Salway, B. (2001) 'Travel, *itineraria* and *tabellaria*', in C. Adams and R. Laurence (eds.), *Travel and Geography in the Roman Empire*, London and New York: 22–66.

Sanderson, M. (1999) 'The classification of climates from Pythagoras to Koeppen', *Bulletin of the American Meteorological Society* 80 (4): 669–673.

Scanlon, T.F. (1988) 'Textual geography in Sallust's *The War with Jugurtha*', *Ramus* 17: 138–175.

Schepens, G. (1997) 'Jacoby's *FGrHist*: Problems, Methods, Prospects', in G.W. Most (ed.), *Collecting Fragments*, Göttingen: 144–172.

Schepens, G. and Delcroix, C. (1996) 'Ancient paradoxography: origin, evolution, production and reception', in O. Pecere and A. Stramaglia (eds.), *La letteratura di consumo nel mondo Greco-Latino* (Atti del Convegno Internazionale, Cassino, 14–17 settembre 1994), Cassino: 373–460.

Schoff, W.H. (1914) Parthian Stations *by Isidore of Charax: An Account of the Overland Trade Route between the Levant and India in the First Century* BC, Philadelphia.

Shaw, B.D. (1981) 'The Elder Pliny's African geography', *Historia* 30 (4): 424–471.

Shcheglov, D. (2005) 'Hipparchus on the latitude of southern India', *GRBS* 45: 359–380.

(2006) 'Eratosthenes' parallel of Rhodes and the history of the system of *climata*', *Klio* 88 (2): 351–359.

Shipley, G.J. (2007) 'A new presentation of *Selected Greek Geographers*', *Syllecta Classica* 18: 241–257.

Sieglin, W. (1893) *Atlas Antiquus*, Gotha.

Sieveking, F. (1964) 'Die Funktion geographischer Mitteilungen im Geschichtswerk des Thukydides', *Klio* 42: 73–179.

Silberman, A. (1993) 'Arrien "Périple du Pont Euxin": Essai d'interprétation et d'évaluation de données historiques et géographiques', *ANRW* 2.34.1: 276–311.

(1995) *Périple du Pont Euxin*, Paris.

Smith, R.R.R. (1988) '*Simulacra gentium*: The *ethne* from the Sebasteion in Aphrodisias', *JRS* 78: 50–77.

Smith, W. and Grove, G. (1872) *An Atlas of Ancient Geography, Biblical and Classical*, London.

Solmsen, F. (1960) *Aristotle's System of the Physical World: A Comparison with His Predecessors*, Ithaca, NY.

Stadter, P.A. (1980) *Arrian of Nicomedia*, Chapel Hill, NC.

Standish, J.F. (1970) 'The Caspian Gates', *G&R* 17: 17–24.

Stoneman, R. (1994) 'Romantic ethnography: Central Asia and India in the Alexander Romance', *AncW* 25 (1): 93–107.

Stückelberger, A. (1994) *Bild und Wort: Das illustrierte Fachbuch in der antiken Naturwissenschaft, Medizin und Technik*, Mainz.

(2007) *Ptolemaios: Handbuch der Geographie*. 2 vols., Basel.

Sulimani, I. (2005) 'Myth or reality? A geographical examination of Semiramis' journey in Diodorus', *SCI* 24: 45–63.

Syme, R. (1987) 'Exotic names, notably in Seneca's tragedies', *Acta Classica* 30: 49–64.

(1988) 'Military geography at Rome', *ClAnt* 7 (2): 227–251.

Talbert, R.J.A. (2005) '*Ubique fines*: Boundaries within the Roman Empire', *Caesarodunum* 39: 91–101.

(2007) 'Author, audience and the Roman empire in the Antonine Itinerary', in R. Haensch and J. Heinrichs (eds.), *Der Alltag der römischen Administration in der hohen Kaiserzeit*, Cologne: 256–270.

(2010) *Rome's World: The Peutinger Map Reconsidered*, Cambridge.

Taub, L. (2009) 'Explaining a volcano naturally: Aetna and the choice of poetry', in L. Taub and A. Doody (eds.), *Authorial Voices in Greco-Roman Technical Writing*, Trier: 125–142.

Thiel, J.H. (1966) *Eudoxus of Cyzicus: A Chapter in the History of the Sea Route round the Cape in Ancient Times,* Groningen.

Thollard, P. (1987) *Barbarie et civilisation chez Strabon: Étude critique des livres III et IV de la* Géographie, Paris.

Thomas, R.F. (1982) *Lands and Peoples in Roman Poetry*, Cambridge.

Thomson, J.O. (1948) *History of Ancient Geography*, Cambridge.

Thorley, J. (1971) 'The silk trade between China and the Roman Empire at its height, circa AD 90–130', *G&R* 18 (1): 71–80.

Tierney, J.J. (1962) 'The map of Agrippa', *Proceedings of the Royal Irish Academy, Sect. C* 63: 151–166.

Torelli, M. (1982) *Typology and Structure of Roman Historical Reliefs*, Ann Arbor, MI.

Toynbee, A. (1969) *Some Problems of Greek History*, Oxford.

Tozer, H.F. (1897) *A History of Ancient Geography*, Cambridge.

Trimble, J. (2007) 'Visibility and viewing on the Severan Marble Plan', in S. Swain, S. Harrison and J. Elsner (eds.), *Severan Culture*, Cambridge: 368–384.

Urlichs, L. (1876) *Die Malerei in Rom vor Caesar's Dictatur*, Würzburg.

Van Paassen, C. (1957) *The Classical Tradition of Geography*, Groningen.

Versluys, M.J. (2002) *Aegyptiaca Romana: Nilotic Scenes and the Roman Views of Egypt*, Leiden.

Veyne, P. (1988) *Did the Greeks Believe in Their Myths? An Essay on the Constitutive Imagination*, Chicago and London (originally published in French 1983).

Visser, E. (1997) *Homers Katalog der Schiffe*, Stuttgart.

Walbank, F.W. (1948) 'The geography of Polybius', *C&M* 9: 155–182.

Watson, B. (1961) *Records of the Grand Historian of China: Translated from the 'Shih Chi' of Ssu-Ma Ch'ien*, vol. 1, New York and London.

Warmington, E.H. (1934) *Greek Geography*, London.

Weerakkody, D.P.M. (1997) *Taprobane: Ancient Sri Lanka as Known to Greeks and Romans*, Turnhout.

Weippert, O. (1972) *Alexander-imitatio und römische Politik in republikanischer Zeit*, Augsburg.

Wheeler, M. (1954) *Rome Beyond the Imperial Frontiers*, London.

Whittaker, C.R. (2000) 'Frontiers', in *Cambridge Ancient History*, vol. 11, Cambridge: 293–319.

Wijsman, H.J.W. (1998) 'Thule applied to Britain', *Latomus* 57 (2): 318–323.

Wittke, A.-M., Olshausen, E. and Szydlak, R. (2007) *Historischer Atlas der antiken Welt (Der Neue Pauly* Suppl. 3), Stuttgart.

(2009) *Historical Atlas of the Ancient World* (*Brill's New Pauly* Suppl. 3), Leiden.

Yee, C.D.K. (1994) 'Reinterpreting traditional Chinese geographical maps', in J.B. Harley and D. Woodward (eds.), *The History of Cartography*, vol. 2.2: *Cartography in the Traditional East and Southeast Asian Societies*, Chicago and London: 35–70.

Yntema, D.G. (2006) 'Ontdekking "oudste kaart" een grap?' *Geschiedenis Magazine* 41: 5.

Zanker, P. (1988) *The Power of Images in the Age of Augustus*, Ann Arbor, MI.

Zimmermann, K. (1999) *Libyen. Das Land südlich des Mittelmeers im Weltbild der Griechen*, Munich.

Zissos, A. (ed.) (2008) *Valerius Flaccus' Argonautica Book 1*, Oxford.

Index